Contents

This coffee falls into your stomach, and straightway there is a general commotion. Ideas begin to move like the battalions of the Grand Army on the battlefield, and the battle takes place ... Similes arise, the paper is covered with ink; for the struggle commences and is concluded with torrents of black water, just as a battle with powder.

Honoré de Balzac (1799–1859),
Treatise on Modern Stimulants (1839)

Introduction

Coffee: A Drink for the Devil is a stirring, invigorating and engaging history of coffee; it blends the facts and ephemera surrounding this globally essential drink to tell the intriguing story of its origins and the history of its discovery, production and consumption through time. In doing so, it shines a fascinating and illuminating light on British, European and North American social history revealing how, as producers or as consumers, we all contributed to the rise and rise of one of the world's most popular drinks and one of its most traded commodities.

Excited Goats Invent Coffee

Legend has it that Kaldi, a lonely goatherd in ninth-century Ethiopia, discovered the energising and invigorating effects of coffee when he saw his goats getting all excited after eating some beans. Kaldi told the abbot of the local monastery about this but the ascetic abbot, however, was far from impressed, and threw the beans into the fire, whence the unmistakeable aroma of what we now know as coffee filled the air. Attracted by this, other monks came to see what was causing such a good smell: the (now) roasted beans were raked from the embers, ground up, and dissolved in hot water. So was made the world's first cup of coffee. Each of the monks found that it kept him awake for hours at a time – just the thing for a man devoted to long hours of prayer. Word spread, and so did the hot drink, with imbibers enjoying their new-found nocturnal lifestyles even as far as the Arabian Peninsula. This story was first published by Antoine Faustus Nairon, a professor of Oriental languages and author of one of the first printed treatises on coffee, *De Saluberrima potione Cahue seu Cafe nuncupata Discurscus* in 1671, some 800 years after the alleged event. 'Kaldi' is still a popular name for coffee shops around the world. The pithily named Yemenite Sufi mystic Ghothul Akbar Nooruddin Abu al-Hasan al-Shadhili also has a claim to the discovery: he spotted coffee-bean-eating birds flying over his village – somewhat energetically. On trying some jettisoned beans, he found himself unusually (psycho-) active.

The Saint from Mocha

An alternative story has us believe that a sheik called Omar, disciple to the Sufi mystic cited above, was in exile from Mocha (Arabia Felix in present-day Yemen). Omar, famous for his ability to cure the sick through prayer, lived in a desert cave near Ousab. Somewhat hungry, Omar chewed some berries only to find them bitter; he roasted them but this only made them hard. Finally he tried boiling them, which resulted in a fragrant brown liquid; like the goats and birds in Ethiopia, the beans gave him unnatural exceptional energy and allowed him to stay awake for days on end. This miracle drug discovery was held in such great awe that he was allowed home and elevated to the sainthood while coffee percolated throughout the Arab world. By the sixteenth century it was the beverage of choice in Persia, Egypt, Syria and Turkey, its reputation as the 'wine of Araby' boosted no end by the thousands of pilgrims visiting the holy city of Mecca each year from all over the Muslim world. Yemeni merchants took coffee home from Ethiopia and began to grow it for themselves. It was prized by Sufis in Yemen who used the drink to aid concentration and as a spiritual intoxication. They also used it to keep themselves alert during their night-time devotions.

Coffee was initially used for spiritual purposes. Muslim dervishes in Yemen grew the shrub in their plots of land, at first making wine from the pulp of the fermented coffee berries. This was known as *qishr* (*kisher* today) and was frequently used during religious ceremonies. The 1,000-year-old tradition lives on today; *Kisher* is a Yemeni hot drink, made of spiced coffee husks, ginger, and cinnamon; being cheaper, it is usually drunk instead of coffee. Thesiger, in his *A Journey Through the Tihama, the 'Asir, and the Hijaz Mountains*, tells us that in Yemen 'ginger coffee is the universal drink and the cup is always filled, a guest being given two cups at once … Qishr, an infusion made from the husks of coffee berries, is also drunk, particularly in the Tihamat al 'Asir'.

Wisely, the Arabs did their utmost to keep their production details a close secret. From the Middle East it soon spread through the Balkans, Italy and to the rest of Europe, east to Indonesia and then west to the Americas, largely through the Dutch.

What Exactly Is Coffee?

Before we go any further, it might be as well to establish just what coffee is. Do you know what a coffee tree looks like? You might recognise a roasted coffee bean when you saw one, but you might not be able to identify an actual coffee tree. A coffee tree can grow more than thirty feet high; it is recognisable by its dark-green, waxy leaves

Coffee *arabica* – what 70 per cent of this book is about.

growing opposite each other in pairs, and the coffee cherries growing along the tree's branches. It takes up to a year for a cherry to mature after the flowering of the fragrant, white blossoms and, because it grows in a continuous cycle, you can often see flowers, green fruit and ripe fruit simultaneously on a single tree. Trees can live up to thirty years and grow in a wide range of climates. They do, however, prefer a rich soil and mild temperatures, with frequent rain and shady sun.

Botanically speaking, the coffee plant is steeped in confusion and controversy. In 1753, Carolus Linneaus described *Coffea arabica* in his *Species Plantarum*. Botanists have argued ever since over its exact classification, no wonder when there are up to 100 species of coffee plants. In today's commercial coffee industry, there are two important coffee species – *arabica* and *canephora*, more commonly known as *robusta*.

So what exactly is *Coffea arabica* ? It is descended from the original coffee trees discovered in Ethiopia, trees which produce a fine, mild, aromatic coffee and make up approximately 70 per cent of the world's coffee production and command the highest prices. Good job, because *arabica* trees are expensive to cultivate: the terrain is often steep and difficult to access. Because the trees are more susceptible to disease than *robusta*, they demand additional care and attention. The higher up they are grown, the better your cup of coffee. The best conditions are between 2,000 to 6,000 feet above sea level, although the critical factor is that temperatures must remain mild, ideally between 59 and 75 degrees Fahrenheit, with about sixty inches of rainfall a year, and frost free. *Arabica* trees are self-pollinating; the beans are flatter and longer than *robusta* and lower in caffeine.

Coffea canephora, *robusta*, is grown in central and western Africa, Indonesia, Vietnam and Brazil; it accounts for the remaining 30 per cent of the world market, although it is on the increase. It is, as the name suggests, more robust and disease resistant, able to withstand warmer climates, preferring temperatures between 75 and 85 degrees Fahrenheit, enabling it to grow at far lower altitudes than *arabica*. *Robusta* beans produce a coffee with about 50 to 60 per cent more caffeine and are mainly used in blends and for instant coffees.

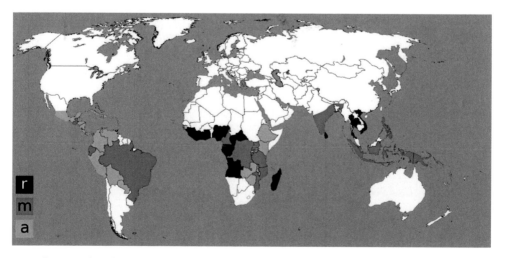

Map showing distribution of coffee *arabica* and coffee *robustica* clustered around the equator. M = both; A = arabica; R = robustica.

1

Ethiopia, the Yemen and How It All Started

Even in its infancy coffee was so powerful a force that it forged a social revolution. Coffee was drunk in the home as a domestic beverage but, more significantly, it was drunk in the ubiquitous public coffee houses – *qahveh khaneh* – which sprang up in villages, towns and cities across the Middle East and east Africa. The coffee houses soon became all the rage and were *the* place to go for a social life. Coffee drinking and conversation were complemented by all manner of entertainment: musical performances, dancing, games of chess and, most crucially, gossiping, arguing and discussing the breaking news of the day, or night. These coffee houses soon became known as 'Schools of the Wise'; this is where you went if you wanted to know what was going on in your world.

According to John Ellis, botanist and zoologist, in his *An Historical Account of Coffee, With an Engraving, and Botanical Description of the Tree*, published in 1774, the first coffee houses in Constantinople were opened in 1475 and patronised by traders from Damascus and Aleppo:

> When two private persons, whose names were Schems and Hekin, the one coming from Damascus, and the other from Aleppo, each opened a Coffee-house ... and sold Coffee publicly, in rooms fitted up in an elegant manner; which were presently frequented by men of learning, and particularly poets and other persons, who came to amuse themselves with a game of chess, or draughts; or to make acquaintance, and pass their time agreeably at a small expence.

Little did they know it but Schems and Hekin had provided the template for the coffee houses of the future, in both the east and the west. The link between coffee and intellectual life had been made. In 1530 the first coffee house in Damascus opened its doors and soon after coffee houses became essential to Ottoman culture and a familiar sight throughout the Empire.

Ellis was trying to promote the cultivation of coffee for export in the West Indies, and gives an account of the plant, fruit and seed. He explains the ideal growing conditions, including an optimum altitude and temperature, and provides detailed descriptions of the various processes by which the seeds are converted into the drink.

From the fifteenth century until the early eighteenth century, the port of Mocha was the principal world marketplace for coffee. *Mocha* beans (also *Sanani* or *Mocha Sanani*

COFFEE MERCHANTS.

THE CUSTOM OF EXTRACTING A DRINK FROM COFFEE BERRIES IS LOST IN ANTIQUITY — THE BEST COFFEE IN THE WORLD IS PRODUCED ON THE MOUNTAINS OF YEMEN, FROM BEING EXPORTED FROM MOCHA IT IS CALLED MOCHA COFFEE, THE ENGRAVING SHOWS A PARTY OF MERCHANTS ON THEIR WAY TO THE COAST WITH THE PRODUCE OF THEIR COFFEE PLANTATIONS

Yemeni coffee merchants.

beans, meaning from Sana'a) have always been famous for their distinctive flavour. English, Dutch, French and Danish East India companies all built factories at Mocha, which remained a major coffee exporting port until the early nineteenth century, even though other outlets had been developed.

Intriguing as the tales of Kaldi and Omar might be, they are, nevertheless, mere legends. The scientific and historical truth, however, is not that different. It is the Oromo people of Ethiopia, northern Kenya, and parts of Somalia who get the credit for discovering coffee and its effects. The Oromos traditionally planted coffee trees on the graves of powerful sorcerers. They believed that the first coffee bush grew from the tears that the god of heaven cried over the corpse of a famous dead sorcerer. The original domesticated coffee plant is also said to have originated from Harar, a town noted for its commercial successes in coffee, weaving, basketry and bookbinding.

Coffee, like alcohol, has a long history of prohibition – attracting fear and suspicion and religious disquiet and hypocrisy. Had the zealots (of all religions) got their way then there would not be very many coffee houses open today. Drinking coffee was banned by jurists and scholars meeting in Mecca in 1511. The opposition was led by the Meccan governor Khair Beg, who was afraid that coffee would foster opposition to his rule by bringing men together and allowing them to discuss his failings. Thus coffee's association with sedition and revolution was born. It was decreed sinful *(haraam)*, but the controversy over whether it was intoxicating or not raged on over the next thirty years until the ban was finally rescinded in 1524 by an order of the Ottoman Turkish Sultan Selim I, with Grand Mufti Mehmet Ebussuud el-İmadi issuing a *fatwa* allowing coffee to be drunk again. Beg was executed for his troubles by command of the Sultan himself, who further proclaimed coffee to be sacred. In Cairo there was a similar ban in 1532; the coffee houses and coffee warehouses there were ransacked. J. E. Hanauer tells us in his *Folk-lore of the Holy Land:*

> The coffee-houses [were] closed, and their keepers pelted with the sherds of their
> pots and cups. This was in 1524, but by an order of Selìm I the decrees of the
> learned were reversed, the disturbances in Egypt quieted, the drinking of coffee
> declared perfectly orthodox.

In the mid-seventeenth century, Murad IV banned coffee in Constantinople, along with alcohol and tobacco; the penalty for breaking the ban was execution. Apparently, Murad patrolled the streets and taverns of Constantinople incognito at night, policing his prohibition by summarily killing civilians who contravened the decree. Even though he was a ruthless and ardent promoter of alcohol prohibition, Murad had a drink problem himself and died from liver cirrhosis in 1640 aged twenty-four.

The Orthodox Ethiopian Church banned coffee drinking until 1889 because it was believed to be a threat to Christianity. However, things changed when Emperor Menilek took a liking to it, and when Abuna Matewos dispelled the belief that it was a uniquely Muslim drink. Today it is the national drink of Ethiopia. In the seventeenth century, coffee was banned in Ottoman Turkey because it was synonymous with rebellious political activity in the west. Further bans and prohibition were to follow as coffee consumption spread throughout Europe and the Americas.

We have to thank the handful of intrepid traders, travellers, explorers, scientists and Orientalists who bravely visited the eastern world from the seventeenth century for our early knowledge and experience of coffee. Pietro della Valle, who was travelling in the east, mentioned coffee in a letter from Constantinople in 1614. Pietro della Valle began his journeys in 1614 on the advice of a doctor, who recommended a long journey as an alternative to suicide after his disastrous love affair. In 1684 coffee merchant Philippe Sylvestre Dufour mentions coffee in a reference to *bunchum* found in the works of the tenth-century CE Persian physician Muhammad ibn Zakariya al-Razi, or Rhazes. In 1587 Abd al-Qadir al-Jaziri compiled a work tracing the history and legal issues relating to coffee entitled *Umdat al safwa fi hill al-qahwa.* Al-Jaziri tells us that one Sheikh Jamal-al-Din al-Dhabhani (d. 1470), a mufti of Aden, was the first to drink coffee in around 1454. He found what everyone by then knew: that 'it drove away fatigue and lethargy, and brought to the body a certain sprightliness and vigour'. Al-Jaziri traces the spread of coffee from *Arabia Felix* to Mecca and Medina in 1414, and then to Cairo in the early sixteenth century, thence to Damascus, Baghdad, reaching Constantinople in 1554. A plethora of coffee houses sprang up in these capitals and in other towns and cities such as Aleppo.

Antoine Galland translated sections of Al-Jaziri as *De l'origine et du progrès du Café. Sur un manuscrit arabe de la Bibliothèque du Roy,* published in Caen in 1699. He too traces the spread of coffee from Arabia Felix to Mecca and Medina, and then to Cairo, Damascus, Baghdad, and Istanbul. Galland was not the only Orientalist fascinated by coffee: Antoine Isaac Silvestre de Sacy edited the first two chapters of al-Jaziri and

An early Cairo coffee house; note the added attraction of the hookah.

included it in the second edition of his *Chrestomathie Arabe* published in Paris in 1826 in three volumes.

In 1583, Leonhard Rauwolf, a German doctor and botanist, described coffee as follows in his *Aigentliche Beschreibung der Raiß inn die Morgenländerin*, the English translation published as *Dr. Leonhart Rauwolf's Travels into the Eastern Countries*, after returning from a two-year trip through the Levant and Mesopotamia from 1573 to 1575. The purpose of the trip was to seek out herbal medicine supplies:

> A very good drink they call Chaube that is almost as black as ink and very good in illness, especially of the stomach. This they drink in the morning early in the open places before everybody, without any fear or regard, out of clay or China cups, as hot as they can, sipping it a little at a time.

This was the earliest printed reference to coffee in Europe and with it was born the endless controversy surrounding alleged medical benefits of the beverage – similar to the squabbling that plagued the consumption and trading of tea and chocolate for centuries.

Venetian traders operating out of Istanbul knew coffee; the Italian physician and botanist Prosper Alpinus noted coffee on his voyage to Egypt in 1580, and included it in *De Medicina Aegyptiorum Libri quatuor* (1591) and *De Plantis Aegypti Liber* (1592) – the earliest published illustration of the coffee plant. The first mention in English (as *chaoua)* appears in *Linschooten's Travels* translated from the Dutch and published in London in 1598. It turns up in *Sherley's Travels* (1601), in a passage describing 'a certain liquor which they call coffe'. In 1603 the English adventurer Captain John Smith, founder of Virginia, refers to 'coffa' in his travelogue.

The keenly protected Arabian monopoly on coffee was well and truly broken by an enterprising Sufi pilgrim from India named Baba Budan around the year 1650. Legend has it that Baba smuggled seven raw coffee beans strapped to his body out of Mocha while on the way back from Hajj – rather like a drug mule today. Then coffee was only exported in roasted or baked form so that no one could grow their own and everyone was obliged to buy from the Yemenis. He brought seven beans because the number seven is considered sacred in Islam. Baba Budan had the coffee seeds planted near the city of Chickmaglur in southern India and they flourished. Baba Budan was revered by both Muslims and Hindus, and his shrine is at Baba Budangiri, Karnataka in India. Baba's coffee trees are the ancestors of most coffee trees growing in the world today, and this region of India today still produces quality coffee beans from Baba's contraband Arabian coffee seeds.

Baba Budan lives on, like Kaldi, as the name of many coffee houses around the world today, and as a blend.

COFFEE HOUSE. CAIRO.

Patrons of a coffee house in Cairo.

The Peacock Hill coffee estate in Pusellawa, Ceylon (modern Sri Lanka) in the mid-1860s. The planter's bungalow is on the left with the drying grounds to the front of it. Coolies can be seen carrying their loads up the steps of the pulping house where machinery is turned by a water wheel. Lithograph 1864 from O'Brien's Views in Ceylon.

A coffee house in Palestine in 1900. It doesn't come any fresher than this.

2

Coffee Comes to Europe:
The Coffee House Revolution

It did not take long for coffee to travel the short distance to the European mainland where it was landed first in Venice on the back of the lucrative trade the city enjoyed with its Mediterranean neighbours. However, it initially met with the suspicion and religious prejudice it had suffered in the Middle East and Turkey. The word on the street, filtering back from intrepid European travellers from the mysterious and mystical lands of the east, was of an equally mysterious, exotic and intoxicating liquor:

> Black in colour and made by infusing the powdered berry of a plant that flourished in Arabia. Native men consumed this liquid all day long and far into the night, with no apparent desire for sleep but with mind and body continuously alert, men talked and argued, finding in the hot black liquor a curious stimulus quite unlike that produced by fermented juice of grape.

To Catholics it was the 'bitter invention of Satan', carrying as it did the whiff of Islam, and it seemed suspiciously like a substitute for wine as used in the Eucharist; in any event it was outlawed. Such was the consternation that Pope Clement VIII had to intervene: he sampled it for himself and decreed that coffee was indeed a Christian as well as a Muslim drink. On tasting it he wittily declared that, 'This devil's drink is so delicious … we should cheat the devil by baptising it!' From then on, coffee has been tagged as the devil's drink, or the devil's cup.

As with tea and chocolate, coffee brought significant baggage when it came to its alleged health benefits. We discuss this long-running and passionate debate and controversy in the chapter on coffee and health; suffice to say that coffee, like those other beverages, had its heretics and its champions in each of the European countries it infiltrated.

The inexorable spread of coffee culture and coffee society is inextricably linked with the establishment and proliferation of the coffee house: *the* place to imbibe. We have already seen how they sprang up in Turkey and the wider Near East as social and convivial meeting places in which to gossip, entertain and be entertained while arguing over the burning issues of the day. The first European coffee house opened in Venice in 1683, the fabulous Caffè Florian, still trading in St Mark's Square today.

Coffee houses were always associated with learning, debate, enlightenment, revolution and the printed word in various forms, such as newspapers, pamphlets, political and

One of the fabulous rooms at the to Caffè Florian in Venice's St Mark's Square. This installation is Bruno Ceccobelli's 'Figli d'api' (1988), comprising 777 individual sculptures made from various materials.

satirical magazines and books. In short, coffee symbolised communication and change. Coffee gets a mention in early botanical, medical, and Orientalist books; its introduction in the west as a result of travel ensured that it was there in books on journeys and exploration.

Published research on coffee started to come thick and fast: in Lyons in 1671, Philippe Sylvestre Dufour published *De l'Usage du Café, du Thé et du Chocolat. Dialogue entre un médecin, un Indien, et un Bourgeois*, the first authoritative study of coffee in French. Paris's first coffee house opened the following year. But the coffee classic was Jean de la Roque's *Voyage de L'Arabie heureuse* published in 1716 – a European bestseller, translated into all of the major languages. In it, la Roque described the coffee tree with engraved plates, and provided a critical discussion of the history of the introduction of coffee into France entitled *Un Mémoire Concernant l'Arbre & le Fruit du Café*. The French edition was followed by one published in Amsterdam the same year; *Gründliche und sichere Nachricht vom Cafée und Cafée-Baum*, a German translation, was published in Leipzig in 1717. The Italian edition was published in Venice in 1721, and English editions in 1726, 1732, and 1742. Another key Italian work dealing with the origins, cultivation, roasting, and preparation of coffee was *Ambrosia Arabica overa della Salutare Bevanda Cafe* by Angelo Rambaldi, published in Bologna in 1691.

Literature, drama and music have their fair share of coffee-related references. This quick journey through the principal coffee houses of Europe will demonstrate these associations.

Austria

Austria was, and arguably still is, the king of coffee house culture. According to the Catholic priest Gottfried Uhlich in a fusion of accounts included in his *History of the Second Turkish Siege*, published 1783, and by Karl Teply in *The Introduction of Coffee in Vienna*, the first coffee house in Austria (and the third in Europe) opened in Vienna in 1683. This was in the immediate aftermath of the crucial Battle of Vienna; it was made possible by using booty which, apart from the usual camels, tents, goats and sheep, also included a good deal of Turkish coffee.

It was King John III Sobieski of Poland himself who presented Jerzy Franciszek Kulczycki, a Polish military officer of Ukrainian origin, with the large amounts of coffee found in the captured camp of Kara Mustafa's army. At the time, many a soldier would have been somewhat perplexed and maybe disappointed by a stash of what was then just a mysterious hill of beans. Not the enterprising and prescient Kulczycki. He opened the coffee house at Schlossergassl near the cathedral. It was called the *Hof zur Blauen Flasche* ('House under the Blue Bottle') and became one of the most popular places in town. Cleverly, Kulczycki always served the mortar-ground coffee in Turkish attire, which only added to the place's mystique and popularity. He remains a Viennese hero and, rightly so, the patron of Viennese café owners even though his café closed soon after his death

Zu den Blauen Flaschen – at the Blue Bottle in 1683. Painted in 1900 from a lithograph by Franz Schams depicting the first coffee house in Vienna.

on 20 February 1694. Every year in October a special Koltschitzky fest is organized by the café owners of Vienna, who decorate their shop windows with Kulczycki's portrait; he is further celebrated with a statue on Vienna's Koltschitzky Street. Kulczycki had played a critical role in raising the siege of Vienna and defeating the Ottomans; a role equalled by the part he played in spreading coffee culture throughout Europe. A less charitable account would have it that Kulczycki had spent two years in an Ottoman jail and knew precisely what coffee really was and duped his superiors into giving him what looked like a hill of worthless beans. Sour grapes, or bad beans, on the part of the Turks?

This was a socially historical event of some significance in itself but Kulczycki went one major step forward in the annals of beverage drinking when he helped to popularise the custom of adding sugar and milk to the coffee. No doubt the Viennese thought Turkish coffee a little on the strong and bitter side for their more delicate tastes. In the very early days, before different coffees were christened and branded with names, customers would select the mixtures of their choice from a colour-shaded chart. To this day, *Wiener Melange* is the typical Viennese coffee, which comes mixed with hot foamed milk and a glass of water and is similar to a cappuccino. The English *Café Vienna* and the French *Café viennois* refer to *espresso con panna* – a coffee topped with whipped cream instead of foamy milk. Ordering a *Wiener Melange* will get you an *espresso con panna* even in Vienna, though this should properly be called a *Franziskaner* (Francisca Monk). The name 'Blue Bottle' has been adopted by a chain of coffee shops and roasters in California.

Now, the fall-out from the battle could not just end with a jubilant cup of coffee. As today, something is often needed to go with that cup of coffee. One culinary story is that the *croissant* was invented at the same time in Vienna to celebrate the defeat of the Ottoman siege, with the traditional shape reflecting the crescents on the Ottoman flags. Many think the *croissant* has French origins but croissants in France are a variant of *Viennoiserie*, introduced to France in 1770 by Marie Antoinette who, of course, was from Vienna.

The bagel too may owe its birth to the Battle of Vienna. The first bagel was given as a gift to King John III Sobieski to mark his victory over the Ottomans. It took the shape of a stirrup to commemorate the victorious charge by the Polish cavalry. There is almost certainly no truth in the legend connecting Marco d'Aviano, the Capuchin friar and advisor to Leopold I, Holy Roman Emperor at the time, with the invention of cappuccino. Capuchin monks split from the Franciscans in the sixteenth century. 'Cappuccino', from the Austrian coffee preparation 'Kapuziner', may possibly refer to the hood of milk on top of the coffee (Italian 'cappuccio' and German 'Kapuze' mean 'hood'), but it probably just reflects the distinctive brown colour of the Capuchin robes.

According to Karl Teply, credit for Vienna's first coffee house goes to an Armenian businessman called Johannes Diodato in 1685. Diodato was a spy in the employ of the Viennese Imperial court; more significantly, he knew all about those dark beans and the equally dark art of making coffee. The Johannes Diodato Park in Wieden, Vienna's fourth district, is dedicated to him.

1685 is also notable for the publication of *Bevanda Asiatica* in Vienna by the Italian naturalist, diplomat and bibliophile Count Luigi Marsili. Isaak de Luca, *der Bürgerlicher Cavesieder,* the 'citizen coffee-maker', was also influential when his Imperial Privilege was granted later. Diodata was followed in 1700 by four Greek-owned coffee houses. Since October 2011 the 'Viennese Coffee House Culture' is listed as an 'Intangible Cultural Heritage' in the Austrian inventory of the National Agency for the Intangible Cultural Heritage, a part of UNESCO. The Viennese coffee house is described as a place 'where time and space are consumed, but only the coffee is found on the bill'.

Viennese coffee houses take some responsibility for coffee houses becoming culture clubs: prominent authors and artists, scientists, and politicians began a tradition of congregating there, and include such celebrities as Arthur Schnitzler, Stefan Zweig, Gustav Klimt, Alfred Adler and Leon Trotsky. In Prague, Budapest, Krakow and Lviv (Lemberg), along with other cities of the Austro-Hungarian Empire, many coffee houses sprang up on the Viennese model. There were coffee houses in Prague, Zagreb, Verona, Trieste, and Venice – characterised by commodious rooms, red velvet seats, and magnificent crystal chandeliers. There were also Viennese cafés in Shanghai to cater for the influx of European immigrants in the late nineteenth and early twentieth century.

The earliest coffee houses could boast several of the characteristics that are still typical of a Viennese-style coffee house today. Waiters served a glass of water with every cup of coffee; the coffee houses provided cards for card games; there were pool tables. In 1720, the Kramersches Kaffeehaus was the first to put out newspapers for its guests to read; warm snacks and alcohol were introduced and served. In 1808, Napoleon's continental blockade of England caused a spike in the price for coffee beans resulting in coffee house owners transforming their businesses into café-restaurants in order to ensure survival. In 1856, women, previously banned, were finally allowed to go in coffee houses; before that the cashiers were the only women permitted.

Coffee houses were seen and used by the Viennese as extensions to their sitting rooms and as an escape from their crowded flats – the coffee houses were comfortable, spacious places where they could socialise with friends and with other people. After the First World War, the first dance cafés opened, playing popular American jazz music. During the 1930s, coffee houses were increasingly used for nefarious black-market activity.

Cafés and coffee houses remain to this day an inextricable part of Vienna's social life. Hotel Sacher Café is world famous for its *Sachertorte*; Café Sperl (1880), was Hitler's café of choice – it was near to the Vienna Academy of Fine Arts, an institution that twice refused to display his work allegedly because his sketches had too few people in them. The Café Sperl has been around since 1880 and was frequented by Archduke Joseph Ferdinand. Café Mozart (1794) has a starring role in *The Third Man*; Café Frauenhuber, Vienna's oldest and Mozart's favourite, is where his final public performance took place on 4 March 1791. Café Landtmann was Sigmund Freud's and Mahler's café of choice. Café Museum became a popular meeting place for painters.

Vienna's Jewish population were always prominent in coffee house society. In 1938 the Nazis spoilt the party when many Jewish coffee house regulars either fled or were arrested. Jewish-owned coffee houses were seized. In 2012, there were about 2,500 coffee houses in Vienna, of which 800 were café restaurants, 900 traditional coffee houses, 680 espresso bars, and 120 café confectioneries.

Czech Republic

In 1863 Café Slavia opened in Prague opposite the National Theatre and was frequented by the city's actors. It was often visited by Franz Kafka, Dvořák and Smetana.

France

We have already met Antoine Galland (1646–1715), an antiquary to Louis IV and a consultant of sorts to the French East India company; he is most famous for translating *A Thousand and One Nights* from the Arabic and for compiling the voluminous *Bibliothèque Orientale*, a huge compendium of information about Islamic culture; he said this about the Muslim association with coffee:

> We are indebted to these great [Arab] physicians for introducing coffee to the modern world through their writings, as well as sugar, tea, and chocolate.

Galland said that he was informed by M. de la Croix, Louis XIV's interpreter, that coffee was brought to Paris by a certain M. Thévenot, keeper of the royal library, who had travelled through the East; in 1657, Thevenot gave some of the beans to his friends, one of whom was de la Croix.

When Suleiman Agha, an ambassador from Sultan Mehmed IV, arrived in Paris with his entourage in 1669, his baggage comprised a large consignment of coffee beans. Not only did he share this with his French and European guests (with waiters decked out in Turkish costume), but he also donated some of the beans to the royal court, thus establishing coffee drinking and other facets of Turkish culture, Turquerie and Orientalism, amongst Parisians. Suleiman visited Versailles where he controversially refused to bow to Louis XIV; the king banished him to Paris where he set up home in a sumptuous house. Suleiman invited Parisian society women home for lavish 'coffee ceremonies', which were imitated in Parisian salons and in high society.

In 1672, an Armenian by the name of Pasqua Rosée set up a coffee stall in Paris; this failed but in 1686 Francesco Procopio dei Coltelli, a man from Palermo, set up his coffee

A poster celebrating the Procope's celebrated clientele.

house in the Rue des Fossés Saint-Germain (present-day Rue de l'Ancienne Comédie). The Café Procope, next to the Ancienne Comédie Française, soon became a rendezvous for the leading intellectuals of the day.

Soon, the café became the Foyer dell'Hôtel des Comédiens du Roy, patronised by *Sa Majesté* (as proclaimed on the façade of the theatre). And so was born the world's first literary café which, for over two centuries, served as a magnet for anyone who was anyone, or, at least, anyone who had aspirations in that direction. Patrons read like a *Who's Who* of the world of belles-lettres, philosophy and of the arts and politics generally – La Fontaine, Voltaire, Rousseau, Beaumarchais, Balzac, Hugo and Verlaine to mention just a few. The modern encyclopedia was born here under the tutelage of Diderot; d'Alembert and Benjamin Franklin came and went; during the Revolution, Robespierre, Danton and Marat conspired here; Bonaparte left his hat here as a pledge. By the end of the eighteenth century there were 700 cafés in Paris; by the mid-nineteenth century, there were 3,000 or so.

The French shared with the Austrians the distinction of providing Europe with the template for the upmarket, intellectual coffee house. The coffee house, along with the cabaret and the salon, made up one side of a unique social triangle: coffee, and the places in which it was served, was seen as a way of mitigating harmful influences of the permissive cabaret, and coffee was considered a check on drunkenness and an effective way to encourage temperance and sobriety. A good coffee house was clean, heated and often furnished with some refinement. They were known as 'Bureaux Académiques' and were inclusive places (for those who could afford the bill) where foreigners, often excluded in other elite establishments, could participate equally in French society.

Coffee soon permeated the quintessentially French salon. We have already met the pioneering Suleiman Agha. Equally influential was Madame de Sévigné, Marie de Rabutin-Chantal, that socialite and letter-writing gossip, who announced in a letter in 1690 that she had finally discovered the 'cappuccino':

> We have good milk and good cows, so we had the idea of skimming the milk and mixing it with sugar and coffee: it is most lovely, and I shall draw great consolation from it next Lent.

She added that Du Bois, her doctor, looked favourably upon coffee as a way of combatting a chest infection or a cold. In a word, concluded Madame de Sévigné, 'this is the *lait cafeté* or the *café laité* of our friend Aliot, the personal physician of the King'. It may be worth remembering, though, that during France's brief flirtation with fashionable chocolate, this was the same woman who gave chocolate a defining role in obstetrics; one of her missives in 1671 tells us that 'The Marquise de Coetlogon took so much chocolate during her pregnancy last year that she produced a small boy as black as the devil, the boy died.'

The French Revolution unofficially began when a radical stood on a table at Café de Foy in Paris to deliver a speech that, two days later, led to the storming of the Bastille in July 1789. This activist was Camille Desmoulins (1760–1794); he was a journalist and politician, a childhood friend of Robespierre and a political ally of Danton and Marat. Café de Foy was just one of the twenty-five or so cafés in the garden of the Palais-Royal frequented by political dissidents; Desmoulins urged the mob to 'take up arms and adopt cockades by which we may know each other'. Other famous cafés include the De Caveau and the Café Mecanique where Mocha coffee was piped direct to guests' cups through the hollow legs in each table.

In 1890 Café de Flore opened in St-Germain-des-Pres and soon becomes a famous meeting place of intellectuals, artists, and film-makers including Giacometti, Picasso, Apollinaire, and Hemingway; this is also where Simone de Beauvoir discussed existentialism with Jean-Paul Sartre.

The Netherlands

The scramble for coffee amongst Europeans to obtain live coffee trees or beans was won by the Dutch in 1616. Pieter van der Broecke, a Dutch merchant, purloined some of the closely guarded coffee bushes from Mocha in Yemen and took them back to Amsterdam. He planted them in the Botanical Gardens where they thrived. A seemingly minor event, but one which had a major impact on the history of coffee.

Van der Broecke's beans produced numerous healthy *Coffea arabica* bushes. In 1658 the Dutch initially used them to instigate coffee cultivation in Ceylon (now Sri Lanka) and later in southern India. They later abandoned these projects to concentrate on their Javanese plantations. Later, the Dutch governor in Malabar (southern India) sent an *arabica* coffee seedling to his colleague in Batavia (now Jakarta) in 1696. It failed due to flooding in Batavia. A second shipment of seedlings was sent in 1699. The plants flourished, and in 1711 the first exports were sent from Java to Europe by the Dutch East India Company (Vereeningde Oost-Indische Company). Within a few years, the Dutch colonies of Java and Suriname were the main suppliers of coffee to Europe. By 1717 things were booming and 2,000 lb were shipped. Indonesia was the first place outside of Arabia and Ethiopia where coffee was widely cultivated.

Batavian coffee sold for three guilders per kilo in Amsterdam at a time when annual incomes in the Netherlands averaged between 200 to 400 guilders. By the end of the

Coffee on the boil in *Flemish Cottage Homes* after the original painting by John A. Heyermans, from a card posted in 1904, published by Raphael Tuck.

eighteenth century, the price had dropped to 0.6 guilders per kilo and coffee drinking spread from the wealthy to the general population. The VOC was the most prominent coffee supplier in the world and it was only in the 1840s that their monopoly was broken by Brazil.

But coffee was less lucrative for the Indonesian farmers who were compelled to grow it under the Cultuurstelsel (Cultivation System), whereby export crops were delivered to government warehouses in lieu of taxes. This corruption, which diverted labour from rice production and caused great hardship for farmers, lives on in an influential novel by Eduard Douwes Dekker (Multatuli), published in 1860 and titled *Max Havelaar: Or the Coffee Auctions of the Dutch Trading Company*. The book was a significant factor in changing Dutch public opinion about Cultuurstelsel and colonialism in general. The name Max Havelaar was adopted by one of the first fair trade organisations.

In the twentieth century and today, the Dutch coffee shop, particularly those in Amsterdam, is not always exactly what it might seem. The principle item on the menu here is not coffee or cakes, but cannabis. Under Dutch drug laws small quantities of cannabis products are permitted to be bought, sold and consumed in regulated and licensed coffee shops. Coffee shops are not allowed to serve alcohol or other drugs, and risk being closed down if found to be in breach. The tolerance towards soft drugs was introduced in the 1970s for the explicit purpose of focusing on the fight against hard drugs. In the Netherlands, 105 of the 443 municipalities have at least one coffee shop.

Many Dutch coffee shops fly green-yellow-red Ethiopian flags and other symbols of the Rastafari movement, or pictures of palm leaves to indicate that they sell cannabis and as a way round the official ban on direct advertising. Dutch coffee houses *not* serving

When is a coffee shop not a coffee shop? When it is in the Netherlands, like this one in Amsterdam. If you want a cup of coffee without the whiff of marijuana then go to a *koffiehuis* or a café.

cannabis are called *koffiehuis* ('coffee house'), while a *café* is the equivalent of a bar. About a third of all visitors to Amsterdam go into one of its 150 or so coffee shops at some point. In the US, the National Organization for the Reform of Marijuana Laws has opened a cannabis-coffee shop in Portland, Oregon. Cannabis is not for sale here, but is distributed freely for consumption on the premises. As of 2014, many such shops have opened in Colorado, earning the state millions of dollars in tax revenues. In Canada there are a growing number of bring-your-own-cannabis coffee shops in Toronto.

Germany

As we have seen, Leonhard Rauwolf made his trip to Aleppo and, in 1582, won for Germany the honour of being the first European country to mention coffee. Adam Olearius (1599–1671), a German orientalist, went to Persia on government business from 1633 to 1636 and when he came back he published an account of his journeys. He said:

> They drink with their tobacco a certain black water, which they callcahwa, made of a fruit brought out of Egypt, and which is in colour like ordinary wheat, and in taste like Turkish wheat, and is of the bigness of a little bean ... The Persians think it allays the natural heat.

In 1637, Johannes Albrecht von Mandelsloh, in his *Oriental Trip*, mentions 'the black water of the Persians called *Kahwe*', saying 'it must be drunk hot'.

German coffee houses were first established in the North Sea ports of Kiel, Bremen (1673) and Hamburg (1679). The Germans first called coffee *Coffee*, the same as us, but during the eighteenth century the French word *café*, transliterated as *Kaffee*, took over. In the eighteenth century the popularity of coffee gradually grew throughout the German states, and was taken up enthusiastically by the ruling classes. Coffee was served at the court of the Great Elector, Frederick William I of Brandenburg, as early as 1675.

Coffee drinking in Germany owes a lot to the English. Northern Germany got an early taste of coffee when an English merchant opened the first coffee house in Hamburg in 1679. Regensburg followed in 1689; Leipzig in 1694; Nuremberg in 1696; Stuttgart in 1712; Augsburg in 1713; and Berlin in 1721. In 1721 Frederick William granted a foreigner the privilege of running a coffee house in Berlin free of all rent. It was known, not surprisingly, as the English Coffee House; for many years, English merchants supplied coffee in northern Germany while Italy supplied southern Germany. Well-known coffee houses in Berlin were the Royal on Behrenstrasse; the Widow Doebbert in the Stechbahn; the City of Rome on Unter-den-Linden; Arnoldi on Kronenstrasse; Miercke on Taubenstrasse; and Schmidt on Poststrasse. Later, Philipp Falck opened a Jewish coffee house on Spandauerstrasse. In the reign of Frederick the Great (1712–1786) there were at least a dozen coffee houses in central Berlin, while in the suburbs coffee was served in the many tents which were set up.

The first coffee periodical, *The New and Curious Coffee House*, was published in Leipzig in 1707 by Theophilo Georgi. In 1721 Leonhard Ferdinand Meisner published the first comprehensive German treatise on coffee, tea, and chocolate in Nuremburg.

As cantor of St Thomas's Church, Leipzig, in 1723-50, Johann Sebastian Bach conducted a musical ensemble at Café Zimmermann where, at some point between 1732 and 1735, he composed the 'Coffee Cantata'. Titled *Schweigt stille, plaudert nicht* BWV

211 (Keep still, stop chattering), it features a young woman, Lieschen, who pleads with her disapproving and stick-in-the-mud father to approve her predilection for drinking coffee, then a new fashion. The libretto, by implication, suggests that some Germans in the eighteenth century took a dim view of coffee drinking; the libretto, by Christian Friedrich Henrici, (Picander), includes the lines,

> Oh! How good the coffee tastes, lovelier than a thousand kisses, milder than Muscat wine. Coffee, coffee, I've got to have it; and if someone wants to get me going, Oh, just give me a cup of coffee!

Indeed, coffee was serious business, even when it came to marriage:

> Lieschen secretly lets it be known: no suitor is to come to my house unless he promises me, and it is also written into the marriage contract, that I will be allowed to make myself a coffee whenever I want one.

And was not without its ability to cause dependence:

> If I couldn't be allowed to drink my little cup of coffee three times a day, in my anguish I will turn into a shriveled-up roast goat.

Indeed, in conclusion, coffee drinking is here to stay:

> A cat will always catch mice, and young girls will stay faithful to their coffee. The mother holds her coffee dear, the grandmother drank it too, so who can tell off the daughters!

In 1723, the Café Zimmermann, or Zimmermannsche Kaffeehaus, was the largest and best Kaffeehaus in Leipzig, and a prestigious focal point for the middle classes and men of taste and style. While women were forbidden from going in coffee houses, they were permitted to attend public concerts at Zimmermann's. The coffee house was at Katharinenstrasse 14, then the most elegant street in Leipzig. There was also a coffee garden in the summer. The four-and-a-half storey Baroque building was built by Doering around 1715 and destroyed by Allied bombing in December 1943.

From 1720 the café was host to the Collegium Musicum, which had been founded by Georg Philipp Telemann when a law student in 1702 and later directed by Bach between 1729 and 1739. Zimmermann charged no fee to the Collegium Musicum for hosting their concerts, nor did the audience have to pay; Zimmermann's expenses were repaid by sales of coffee. The concerts ended with Zimmermann's death in 1741. A contemporary French classical music ensemble, *Café Zimmermann*, formed in 1998, is named after the coffee house.

During the second half of the eighteenth century, coffee began to be drunk in German homes and replaced flour-soup and warm beer at breakfast tables.

Meanwhile it was not just the coffee that was brewing. In Prussia and Hanover there was trouble over the economic impact of coffee. Without coffee-producing colonies of his own, Frederick was obliged to import all his coffee from other countries at what he

JOHANN
SEBASTIAN
BACH
*Concerts avec plusieurs
instruments (vol. 1 à vi)*
Intégrale

CAFÉ ZIMMERMANN

CD cover for one of the Baroque ensemble Café Zimmerman's CDs, named after the famous coffee house where Bach's Collegium Musicum probably played.

considered great expense. On 13 September 1777, Frederick issued a bizarre coffee and beer manifesto:

> It is disgusting to notice the increase in the quantity of coffee used by my subjects, and the amount of money that goes out of the country in consequence. Everybody is using coffee. If possible, this must be prevented. My people must drink beer. His Majesty was brought up on beer, and so were his ancestors, and his officers. Many battles have been fought and won by soldiers nourished on beer; and the King does not believe that coffee-drinking soldiers can be depended upon to endure hardship or to beat his enemies in case of the occurrence of another war.

The edict eventually failed to have much effect and Frederick resorted to his former policy of selective elitism. In 1781 he created a royal monopoly in coffee, and forbade its roasting except in royal roasting establishments, only making exceptions for the nobility, the clergy, and government officials and rejecting all applications for coffee-roasting licences from the lower orders. The elite, of course, were obliged to buy their coffee from the government, who had massively increased the price to ensure a handsome margin for the crown. A coffee-roasting licence became an emblem of the upper class while the poorer classes resorted to obtaining their coffee by stealth in the black market. The final option was to make ersatz coffee from barley, wheat, corn, chicory and dried-fig substitutes. Frederick thereby made coffee a drink for the elite by raising the taxes; soon all the German courts had their own coffee roasters, coffee pots, and coffee cups. Much of this was beautifully produced in Meissen. The rich followed suit while the disadvantaged poor were told to abstain because coffee caused sterility. Many a German doctor supported this deceptive campaign, which also decreed that women who drank coffee must abandon all thoughts of child-bearing. Bach's *Coffee Cantata* is the famous protest against such duplicitous misinformation.

Frederick's 1781 edict was known as the 'Déclaration du Roi concernant la vente du café brûlé'; the coffee *regie* (revenue) was deputed to a Frenchman, Count de Lannay, who pursued his task with such vigour that it became something of a persecution. His many deputies, mainly discharged wounded soldiers, spied on the people day and night, following their noses to detect the smell of roasting coffee. The despised spies received 25 per cent of the fine collected and were called 'coffee-smellers'.

Things were even more draconian and sinister in Cologne. In 1784 the elector, Maximilian Frederick, bishop of Münster, issued a manifesto that said:

> To our great displeasure we have learned that in our Duchy of Westphalia the misuse of the coffee beverage has become so extended that to counteract the evil we command that four weeks after the publication of this decree no one shall sell coffee roasted or not roasted under a fine of one hundred dollars, or two years in prison, for each offense. Every coffee-roasting and coffee-serving place shall be closed, and dealers and hotel-keepers are to get rid of their coffee supplies in four weeks. It is only permitted to obtain from the outside coffee for one's own consumption in lots of fifty pounds. House fathers and mothers shall not allow their work people, especially their washing and ironing women, to prepare coffee, or to allow it in any manner under a penalty of one hundred dollars. All officials and government employees, to avoid a penalty of one hundred gold florins, are called upon closely to follow and to keep a watchful eye over this decree. To the one who reports such persons as act contrary to this decree shall be granted one-half of the said money fine with absolute silence as to his name.

It was a complete failure. Meanwhile, the Duke of Württemberg was even more venal than King Frederick. He sold the exclusive rights of running coffee houses in Württemberg to Joseph Suess-Oppenheimer, an unscrupulous financier. He in turn sold the individual coffee-house licences to the highest bidders, and made a considerable fortune as a result. He was the first 'coffee king'.

The first drip coffee maker was patented in 1908 by a Dresden woman, Melitta Bentz. Bentz hankered after a tastier and more efficient way to brew her home-made coffee and had tired of the old choice between a Turkish coffee with grounds in the bottom of the cup, or with the grounds messily strained out through a dishcloth. Bentz knew she could improve on this technique, so she took a piece of blotting paper from her son's school exercise book, inserted the paper inside a metal pot punctured with a nail with holes at the bottom, and so invented a container with disposable paper filters. She patented it as the 'Filter Top Device Lined with Filter Paper'. Bentz went into business with less than 1 Deutschmark and established a company, Melitta (which is still trading), to sell her wonderful new product. She hired a tinsmith to make the machines and sold 1,200 at the 1909 Leipzig fair. In 1910, the company won a gold medal at the International Health Exhibition. When the First World War broke out, her company, like many others, had a difficult time: metals were requisitioned for use in Zeppelin construction, her husband was conscripted to Romania, paper was rationed, and coffee beans imports evaporated due to the British blockade. During this time Melitta supported her family by selling cardboard cartons.

Nevertheless, by 1928 Melitta was on the up again with eighty workers working double-shifts. In 1929 the company moved to Minden, by which time 100,000 filters had

Melitta Bentz's first coffee filter, now in the Deutschen Hygiene Museum Dresden.

been produced. In the 1930s, Melitta revised the original filter, tapering it into the shape of a cone and adding ribs. This created a larger filtration area, allowing for improved extraction of the ground coffee. A few years later, the familiar cone-shaped filter papers that fit inside the tapered filter top were introduced. She transferred the majority stake in Melitta-Werke Aktiengesellschaft to her sons Horst and Willi in 1932, but stayed in touch with some enlightened acts of industrial philanthropy: Christmas bonuses, increasing holidays from six to fifteen days per year, and reducing the working week to five days. Bentz established the company's 'Melitta Aid' system, a social fund for employees. After the end of the Second World War, the main factory was requisitioned by the Allies until 1957, but by 1948 the production of filters and paper had resumed, and by the time of Melitta's death in 1950 the company was worth 4.7 million Deutschmarks. Melitta is still headquartered in Minden.

Today in Germany a long-standing tradition lives on; in between lunch and dinner, there is still sometimes a short break for a social gathering around cake and a cup of coffee or tea. This is known as *Kaffee und Kuchen*, *Kaffeetrinken* or *Kaffeeklatsch* and most commonly takes place with friends and family on Sunday afternoon between 3 and 5 p.m. It can happen in the home or in a café or in a *Konditorei* (confectionery shop). It stems from the time when women were not allowed in the coffee houses and, not to be outdone, began organising private *Kaffeekränzchen*, or coffee parties, in their own homes. A less-treasured relic of the past is *Blümchenkaffee*, the hated weak coffee served when money or supplies were tight. It means 'flower coffee' – an indication that, while drinking a cup of watery coffee, you can see the flowers painted at the bottom of your cup.

In 1903 Ludwig Roselius, a German importer of coffee, serendipitously discovered that a batch of Nicaraguan coffee beans that had been soaked in water during transit had lost most of their caffeine but not their taste. Roselius's assistant Karl Wimmer then worked out how to remove the caffeine from coffee beans without spoiling the coffee's taste when brewed by using steam and chemical solvents. Later, a water-only process was developed. The first decaffeinated coffee was thus produced. Roselius marketed the coffee under the brand name Sanka, which comes from the French phrase 'sans caffeine'.

Today, on average Germans drink 150 litres of coffee per year – more than beer, wine or mineral water. With over 1,000 shops, Hamburg-based Tchibo is one of Germany's biggest chains. The company was founded in 1949 by Carl Tchillinghiryan and Max Herz; the name Tchibo is an abbreviation for Tchilling and Bohnen (beans, i.e. coffee beans). In the early years, Tchibo focussed on the mail order supply of freshly roasted coffee beans, processed in the company's own roasting facility in Hamburg.

Italy

The place where it all started for Europe, in Venice, where there were soon over 200 coffee houses along its canals The reputation of this wonderful new drink soon spread to Verona, Milan and Turin where typically elegant new coffee houses were built. Napoleon got close to a perfect description when he called St Mark's Square and its many coffee houses the best drawing room in Europe. The early days of the Caffè Florian are recounted on the website 'The Procuratie' www.venetia.it/s_proc_eng/.htm from which this interesting and amusing extract is taken:

> The New and Old Procuratie, bordering the Square, was the offices of the 9 Procurators, the most important citizens of Venice after the Doge. They were controlling the Square, the Basilica and the 6 sections of the city, called *sestieri*. In 1585 the Venetian ambassador to Istanbul told the Senate that the Turkish were drinking a hot black drink, made by a seed called Kahavè and that people had difficulty in falling asleep after drinking this beverage. This seed was brought back to Venice and in 1638 it was roasted, ground and sold at an expensive price from a special caffè shop which was located directly under the Procuratie. In a short time the caffè shops opened all of the city and by the end of the next century there were 24 such caffès in St Mark's Square alone. These caffès soon became the favorite place among intellectuals to meet and drink coffee. Gambling, another favorite past time of the Venetian nobility also went on in the caffès.
>
> The popularity of these places grew more and more, and in 1720 one of the most elegant: 'Caffè alla Venezia trionfante' opened its doors. This *Caffè of the Triumphant Venice* was a popular meeting point for both foreign and national high society … The caffè's first owner was Floriano Francesconi and therefore the caffè was affectionately called 'Florian'. In 1775 G. Quadri decided to open a new caffè shop in front of the Florian on the opposite side of the Square and promised to serve only real Turkish Café. For a long time the shop had a bad reputation, driving the owner to near bankruptcy, but in 1830 the nobility recognized the Caffè Quadri as having fine service and quality coffee and its reputation for quality remains today … The Venetians were also well known for their love of beautiful women and love affairs were frequent and legendary. Giacomo Casanova became one of the most legendary lovers of Venetian origin but other lesser known lovers soon filled the State orphanages with their children. Many of these love affairs had their start in the caffès of St Mark's Square so in 1767 the government prohibited women from frequenting caffès. However, Casanova couldn't resist the charms of the women who strolled

The old and the new Caffè Florian

Life, and impeccable service, goes on at the Caffè Florian despite a flooded St Mark's Square.

about the Square and under the porticos of the Procuratie. He was placed in 'Piombi', the prison, by State Investigators because of his lascivious and anti-religious habits.

Caffè Florian is the world's oldest coffee house in continuous operation; it opened with two simple furnished rooms. As in Vienna and Paris the Caffè had some eminent patrons, including the playwright Carlo Goldoni, Goethe and Casanova. Later Lord Byron, Marcel Proust, and Charles Dickens were frequent visitors. As in Vienna, newspapers were a feature; Florian was one of the few places where Gasparo Gozzi's early newspaper *Gazzetta Veneta* could be found.

In the mid-eighteenth century the Florian expanded to four rooms. In 1858, despite public outcry, the caffè was refurbished and it was then that the rooms were splendidly and opulently decorated and given the names by which they are still known. The *Sala degli Uomini Illustri* (Hall of the Illustrious Men) featured paintings by Giulio Carlini of ten notable Venetians including Goldoni, Marco Polo, Titian, Andrea Palladio, Benedetto Marcello and Vettor Pisani. In the *Sala del Senato* the walls are decorated with scenes from the art world with the theme 'Progress and Civilisation instructing the Nations'. The *Sala Cinese* and *Sala Orientale* take their inspiration from the Far East with paintings of lovers and scantily clad exotic women painted by Pascuti. The *Sala delle Stagioni* (Hall of the Seasons) or *Sale degli Specchi* (Hall of Mirrors) was decorated by Rota with the figures of women representing the four seasons. The *Sala Liberty*, added at the beginning of the twentieth century, is decorated with hand-painted mirrors.

From 1893, the Florian became home to the *Esposizione Internazionale d'Arte Contemporanea* (International Exhibition of Contemporary Art), a revolving display of work from the artists of the time, known today as the Biennale di Venezia, and the rooms of the Florian were decorated with the works of artists, sculptors, photographers and cartoonists. In 2003 Irene Andessner added *Le Donne Illustri* (The Illustrious Women), ten portraits of notable women of Venice, to the Hall of the Illustrious Men. Many of the Florian's private collection are loaned to art museums around the world. Music is played at the Florian from April to October. Recently, Florian branched out and opened a caffè in Florence; they have extended the franchise to include branches in Abu Dhabi, in Harrods in London, and in Dubai International Financial Centre.

In Rome, the first coffee-shop was allegedly opened by a Jewish resident in 1650 on the Campus Martius; this caused the usual outrage, self-interest and consternation. In 1674 the chief doctor Ludovico Martoli reacted as follows in a public declaration:

> This type of bean, that comes from abroad and is popularly known as coffee has only recently arrived in Rome, where it is being sold for public consumption. It is ordered that nobody, of any nationality or status may sell or administer this coffee to anybody, unless it has first been approved by us and given written permission. The penalty for any infringement of this law is a fine of 25 scudi.

The owner's twelve sons by two wives scotched rumours claiming that coffee had an adverse effect on a man's virility.

The Antico Caffé Greco in Rome – named after its Greek owner and opened in 1760 can boast an equally impressive roll call of patrons, including Stendhal, Goethe, Byron, Liszt, Keats, Ibsen, Hans Christian Andersen, Mendelssohn, Wagner and Casanova.

The beautiful Pedrocchi Café was founded in the eighteenth century in Padua, and is famous for its role in the 1848 riots against the Habsburg monarchy, as well as for being popular with artists and writers from Stendhal to Lord Byron to Dario Fo.

Turin's oldest surviving coffee house opened in 1763 and was named Caffè Al Bicerin (literally *the little cup* in the local Piemontese dialect), situated on Piazza della Consolata, and is home to the traditional drink of Turin, the 'Bicerin', the exact recipe for which remains a secret. It is made of espresso, drinking chocolate and whole milk served layered in a small rounded glass. The beverage has been known since the eighteenth century and was much beloved of Alexandre Dumas around 1852. It is believed to be based on the seventeenth-century drink 'Bavareisa'; the key difference being that in a bicerin the three components are carefully layered in the glass rather than being mixed together. Once frequented by the aristocracy, including Puccini, Cavour and Dumas, the tiny and ancient coffee house has only eight marble-topped tables.

> Turin's Cafés were once a male preserve, meeting places for merchants and the literati. Bicerin was different: open since 1763, it has always been owned and run by women. In time, it became fashionable for women to take their coffee there after receiving communion at the Santuario of the Consolata across the piazza.
> Kieran Cooke in the *Financial Times*

Friedrich Nietzsche was always partial to a glass of bicerin. When he first drank it he reputedly exclaimed, 'Scorching hot, but it's delicious!'

In the picture are Mrs Cavalli and her daughter in front of the café. She was the owner up to the 1970s over two generations; after that Mrs Maritè Costa's family own the business. This picture dates to the mid-1930s.

Caffé al Bicerin in the snow. The blue Bicerin brand mark can be seen on either side of the window.

A suitably atmospheric photo of the Caffè Fiorio in the 1950s.

A typical day in the Caffè Fiorio in the nineteenth century.

The Caffè Fiorio in Turin was founded in 1780 when it soon it became the place to go for the artistic, intellectual and political classes of the capital of the Kingdom of Sardinia. It was known as 'the café of the Machiavellis and of the pigtails (*codini*)' – a term applied to reactionary politicians, apparently with reference to pre-revolutionary French hairstyles.

One of the most iconic images emblematic of the importance of coffee in Italian society is the 'macchinetta', the instantly recognisable aluminium stove-top percolator, designed and produced by Bialetti in 1933.

Italy still insists on coffee-drinking decorum and inventiveness. Most Italians never order a cappuccino after 11 a.m. for cappuccino is a breakfast beverage; no decent restaurant will serve a milk-based coffee after dinner. Never ask for an espresso, simply request, '*un caffè, per favore*' and you will receive a short, strong black shot accompanied by a glass of water for palate cleansing. In Trentino, ask for a 'cappuccino Viennese' and you'll get a frothy coffee with chocolate and cinnamon. In the Marche region, stop for a 'caffè anisette' for an aniseed-flavoured espresso, in Naples enjoy coffee flavoured with hazelnut cream and, while in Sicily, indulge in a 'caffè d'u parrinu' – an Arabic-inspired coffee flavoured with cloves, cinnamon and cocoa powder. Finally, a nice Neapolitan tradition is the practice of 'caffè sospeso', suspended coffee: this is where you pay for two coffees but only drink one, leaving the other for a stranger to enjoy for free.

Outside the Greco in Rome in the 1990s.

3

Coffee Comes to England: The Seventeenth-Century World Wide Web

Francis Bacon, in his *Historia Vitae et Mortis*, published in 1623, warned his readers against the dangerous properties of coffee, suggesting that there was some familiarity with the beverage well before the establishment of any known coffee house in Britain. Travellers introduced coffee to England as a socialising beverage; before that it had been taken mainly for its supposed medicinal properties. The first botanical description of coffee in English was published by Parkinson in *Theatrum Botanicum* in 1640. As in other countries, coffee drinking was associated with coffee houses. According to Samuel Pepys, England's first coffee house was established by a Jewish gentleman called Jacob at the Angel in the parish of St Peter in the East, Oxford. The building is now known as 'The Grand Café'. Originally established in 1650, the café still trades today, and its longevity is commemorated by a plaque on the wall. Given Oxford's reputation for academic excellence and the scholarly enquiring and enlightenment that pervaded the city, it seems only natural that coffee society be born here, especially given how the coffee houses were to develop into informal, refined havens of education, cauldrons of polemic, debate and discussion.

Over the years, the site has been a coffee shop, an inn, a hotel, a grocer's shop, a Co-op, a marmalade factory and a Post Office. The Grand Café as it is now re-opened in the mid-1990s. The earliest record found of this site in Oxford comes in 1391, when an inn called 'Tabord' was leased by St. John's Hospital where Magdalen College is today. In 1510 it was extended and expanded and renamed 'The Angel', becoming Oxford's premier coaching inn. The horses were grazed in the meadow next to Magdalen College – hence 'Angel Meadow'. Anthony Wood corroborates Pepys in his *The Life and Times of Anthony Wood, Antiquary of Oxford 1632–1695*:

> This year [1651] Jacob the Jew opened a coffey house at the Angel in the parish of S. Peter, in the East Oxon; and there it was by some, who delighted in noveltie, drank. When he left Oxon, he sold it in Old Southampton buildings in Holborne neare London, and was living in 1671.

The building is steeped in the history of beverages and good things that go with them. In 1867 Frank Cooper inherited the family business and expanded the shop, combining both Number 83 and 84. In 1874, his wife Sarah Jane had been making marmalade in the family kitchen and hit on the idea of selling the 'overstocks', and a bestselling brand was born: 'Oxford Marmalade'. In 1900 Frank Cooper opened the famous Jam Factory in Park End Street. In 1919 the Twining brothers of tea fame took over the shop premises until 1939 and in 1984 the Coopers set up a shop and museum to showcase their world-famous marmalade.

Oxford's Queen's Lane Coffee House was opened in 1654 by Cirques Jobson and became a popular haunt of the many local scholars; it still trades on the corner of Queen's Lane and the High. John Evelyn and Christopher Wren were among the patrons of Oxford coffee houses.

The emergence of the Oxford coffee house happened to coincide with the emergence of new, exciting academic disciplines, including experimental philosophy. In the mid-1650s a number of scholars took to meeting regularly in these coffee houses under the management of an apothecary named Arthur Tillyard. They debated the new ideas transforming natural philosophy (science) and the mathematical sciences. Peter Staehl put on experimental displays there. The scholars drifted to London in 1660, homing in on the coffee houses that had just started to open in the capital, eventually re-surfacing as the Royal Society. What began in Oxford and London would go on to influence scientific progress throughout Western Europe.

London's first coffee house opened in 1652 in St Michael's Alley, Cornhill, near to St Michael's churchyard. It was run by Pasqua Rosée, whose portrait was on the sign outside and whom we have already met in Paris. The previous year, Thomas Hodges, a grocer and Turkey merchant, had taken in the young draper and Levant merchant Daniel Edwards as a lodger, and Edwards was intent on marrying Hodges' daughter. Edwards had come back from Izmir with Rosée, bringing with him everything Levantine merchants were noted for: hard work, Puritan politics, and coffee drinking. Coffee proved so popular *chez* Hodges that Edwards and Hodges set Rosée up in a stall in St Michael's churchyard to sell coffee to the public. Christopher Bowman, apprenticed to Hodges, joined Rosée and they moved across St Michael's Alley to better premises in 1656. Bowman's coffee house was successful until 1662. The coffee house was also the Jamaica Wine House, known locally as 'the Jampot' and as the Turk's Head. Contemporary advertisements in pamphlets and newspapers refer to coffee as 'the right Turkie berry'. A promotional handbill, *The Vertue of the Coffee Drink*, now resides in the British Museum.

Pepys visited the coffee house on 10 December 1660:

[Col. Slingsby] and I in the evening to the Coffee House in Cornhill, the first time that ever I was there, and I found much pleasure in it, through the diversity of company and discourse.

The blue plaque reads 'Here stood the first London Coffee house at the sign of the Pasqua Rosée's Head 1652'. Pepys went again on New Year's Day 1664 when he was able to gossip scandalously about a 'very rich widow, young and handsome' and the 'great courtiers that already look after her. Her husband not dead a week yet.' In between these visits, on 16 January 1663, he reports, 'There being with us Captain Brewer, the paynter, who tells me how highly the Presbyters do talk in the coffeehouses still, which

I wonder at.' He refers to the Rose (3 February 1663), later known as Will's Coffee-House, after William Urwin, the landlord, the place where Dryden had a chair reserved. It was on the west side of Bow Street, and at the corner of Russell Street. He says:

> In Covent Garden to-night, going to fetch home my wife, I stopped at the great Coffee-house' there, where I never was before; where Dryden the poet (I knew at Cambridge), and all the wits of the town, and Harris the player, and Mr. Hoole of our College. And had I had time then, or could at ether times, it will be good coming thither, for there, I perceive, is very witty and pleasant discourse. But I could not tarry, and as it was late, they were all ready to go away.

Dryden visited Will's every day; the mornings were devoted to writing at home, and the rest of the day was spent at the coffee house till late. In 1679, an outrage:

> Mr. Dryden, the poet, comeing from the coffee-house in Covent Garden, was set upon by three or four fellows, and very soarly beaten, but likewise very much cutt and wounded with a sword. It is imagined that this has happened to him because of a late satyr that is laid at his door, though he positively disowned it.

The hired hooligans were in the pay of Lord Rochester, livid at a publication that, although not by Dryden, had been printed with a title page which suggested that it was his work.

On 10 February 1664 Pepys stops off for a coffee and a quick chat on the way home, 'Thence homewards, calling a little at the Coffee-house, where a little merry discourse, and so home'; the 12th sees him in a coffee house again, twice. The entry for 24 February might suggest that the coffee house had become part of his daily routine: 'Thence by water [from Somerset House] to the Coffee-house, and there sat with Alderman Barker talking of hempe and the trade.' Indeed, on the 29th we find him going to the 'Change, and thence to a Coffee-house with Sir W. Warren, and did talk much about his and Wood's business, and thence homewards. Morat's Coffee House or Turk's Head in Exchange Alley is mentioned in Pepys' entry for 28 May 1663 – Pepys notes the Coffee

A typical coffee house scene as depicted on this mural from the 1940s, in the dining room at Cadbury's Bournville factory.

Club of the Rota in 1659, as a forum for exchange of republican views which met in the Turk's Head.

For Pepys – and many other literate men – the coffee house was his newspaper, his internet: he refers to the latest news of the conflict with the Dutch, 'the comet seen in several places' (15 December 1664) and the 'threat of the plague growing upon us… and of remedies against it' (24 May 1665). It was his encyclopedia: in his entry for 3 November 1663 Pepys refers to diverse discussions on the Roman Empire, the difference between being awake and dreaming, and a discourse on insects.

> At noon to the Coffee-house, and there heard a long and most passionate discourse between two doctors of physique, of which one was Dr. Allen, whom I knew at Cambridge, and a couple of apothecarys; these maintaining chymistry against them Galenicall physique.

London's second coffee house opened in 1656 as the Rainbow, near Temple Bar, in Fleet Street; it also served tea and chocolate and was run by a man named Farr. He was arraigned on charges of causing a nuisance by his neighbours who complained of the strange smell of roasting coffee:

> We present James Farr, barber, for making and selling of a drink called coffee, whereby in making the same he annoyeth his neighbours by evill smells; and for keeping of fire for the most part night and day, whereby his chimney and chamber hath been set on fire, to the great danger and affrightment of his neighbours.

The plague years (1664–5) and the Great Fire (1666) failed to diminish the surging popularity of these new social establishments, but they were not without their opponents. Pamphlets such as 'A Coffee Scuffle' (1662) or 'The Character of a Coffee House … by an Eye and Ear Witness' (1665) gave an alternative view of the social, cultural and even medical questions raised by coffee. One 1681 play had the line 'In a coffee house just now among the rabble, I bluntly asked, which is the treason table?'

In 1659, political philosopher James Harrington (1611–77) – whose *Oceana* (1656) celebrated republicanism – organised regular debates at Miles' Coffeehouse in Westminster. Here soldiers, politicians, and the man in the street avidly discussed and argued over the history and philosophy of government. The Rota, as Harrington called this forum, both generated new knowledge and, more importantly, exemplified a new way of proposing, debating and discussing issues in general and in public. Aubrey gives a vivid account of the room at the coffee house where the club met, with its

> large oval-table, with a passage in the middle for Miles to deliver his coffee. About it sat his disciples and the virtuosi. Here we had (very formally) a ballotting box, and ballotted how things should be carried by way of Tentamens. The room was every evening full as it could be crammed.

'Tentamen' was a Dutch word for a short examination.

The Restoration, of course, brought the republican meetings at Miles's to an abrupt end and Harrington was committed to the Tower to reflect at his leisure on the merits or otherwise of ideal commonwealths.

What compelled men to congregate in coffee houses? It was surely something more than celebrating the Restoration and its restored liberation and freedoms, something more than escaping the home and family, or the drudgery of the workplace. Dispensing and receiving information – news, tittle-tattle, ships' movements, commodity prices, rumour and scandal – were the draw to the coffee house. Never before had there been such a focal point for what was an information revolution. Word of mouth, newspapers and pamphlets all conspired in these places to provide a font of knowledge about all manner of things: the coffee house was the Google, the Wikipedia, the World Wide Web of its day.

During the Protectorate the news publications were distilled into one official newsbook – the state-controlled sixteen-page *Publick Intelligencer* published every Monday, and on a Thursday in a digest format, *Mercurius Politicus*. What we now know as foreign correspondents would file their reports from such cities as Lübeck, Cleve, Amsterdam and Copenhagen, and occasionally Bristol, Westminster, Scotland and Ireland. Domestic news, however, was thin on the ground and lost among the official declarations, book advertisements and announcements regarding errant horses. Handwritten newsletters (typically 800 words or so) augmented the official publications in the coffee houses with mainly foreign news. The London Bills of Mortality were very popular as their human interest element, tabloid character if you like, ignited conversation and comment; their personal tragedies were also syndicated in the regional press and their statistics used pragmatically to fashion personal strategies relating to such things as plague avoidance.

The free weekly advertisers started to appear around 1657, and these too would have been available in the coffee houses. Marchamont Nedham's *Publick Adviser* was probably the first: he was originally Cromwell's press agent and an active pamphleteer. The people at the *City Mercury* were the first to distinguish between circulation and readership, boasting a 1:20 ratio – assisted, no doubt, by free availability in the coffee houses. Advertisements reflected all life: you could attend auctions, buy birdcages, telescopes, wheelchairs, slaves, shoe polish, wigs, positions in the church. You could even follow the searches for runaway wives and absent apprentices.

7 November 1665 saw a revolution in newspaper publishing when the official government newssheet was remodelled and published twice weekly, first as the *Oxford Gazette* and then as the *London Gazette*. Again, the success of this major publishing event was assisted by its ubiquity in the coffee houses where the avid readers – the Westminster wannabes – could pride themselves on being privy to the same news as government officials and diplomats, British and foreign. The *London Gazette* was our first newspaper and provided the template for all subsequent newspapers, and it was there for all to read in the coffee houses. Foreign newspapers were available too, especially Dutch, so that anyone who could translate them would get a Dutch-eye view of affairs in England, just as the English did of affairs in the Netherlands from scanning the London papers.

As with tea and chocolate, coffee attracted its fair share of vitriolic opposition. Much of this came through the important and influential medium of pamphlets published in coffee houses; one example is *A Cup of Coffee, or Coffee in its Colours*, published in 1663:

For men and Christians to turn Turks and think
To excuse the crime, because 'tis in their drink!

Pure English apes! ye might, for aught I know,
Would it but mode learn to eat spiders too.
Should any of your grandsires' ghosts appear
In your wax-candle circles, and but hear
The name of coffee so much called upon,
Then see it drank like scalding Phlegethon;
Would they not startle, think ye, all agreed
'Twas conjuration both in word and deed?

Pamphlets covered a whole range of issues. A random selection of the many pamphlets and broadsheets published from Tom's Coffee House at 17 Russell Street, Covent Garden, includes expatiations on such diverse topics as dentistry (*A Dissertation on Artificial Teeth in General*, in French and English), medicine (*A Problem Concerning the Gout*), the Treaty of Utrecht, France, Hull, slavery (*A Proposal for the Better Supplying of Churches in or Plantations And for Converting the Savage Americans to Christianity*) and astrology. Politics, science, medicine and religion were, not surprisingly, the most popular subjects. *An Anatomical Account of the Elephant Accidentally Burnt in Dublin* printed in 1681 must have been fascinating, as indeed *The Cudgel, or a Crab-tree Lecture by Hercules Vinegar Esq* (1742). Even Boswell was a customer.

The Exclusion Crisis, which took place between 1679 and 1681, saw a high point in pamphlet publishing when twenty a day were being churned out. The Exclusion Bill sought to exclude the king's brother and heir, James, Duke of York, from the thrones of England, Scotland and Ireland because he was Roman Catholic.

Satirical prints (forerunners of the political cartoon) and broadside ballads also found a home in the coffee houses, contributing much to the torrid debates and discussions. Early day *Financial Times* and *Lloyd's List* were also must-have staples in the coffee house reference library. Publications gave daily news of bills of entry (*London, Imported*, from 1660); commodity price lists (*Prices of Merchandise in London*, from 1667); stock prices and exchange rates (the twice-a-week *Course of the Exchange* from 1698); and shipping lists and movements (*Lloyd's News* from 1697). Indeed, Lloyd's of London grew from Edward Lloyd's coffee house in Tower Street in the 1680s, moving in 1692 to Abchurch Lane off Lombard Street. Lloyd made special arrangements to receive news of shipping activity there and Lloyd's List, Lloyd's insurance institution, as well as the Register of Shipping, originated in his coffee house. It is easy to see why the coffee house became a commercial centre and a trading floor. People would go to the Virginian and Maryland (later the Baltic) to subscribe to new investment schemes in Russia. The daily *Votes of the House of Commons* appeared in 1688, anticipating *Hansard*, and recording speeches and resolutions. Cutting-edge science could be read about in 1665's *Philosophical Transactions* – the equivalent of today's *Nature* and *New Scientist*. Literary tastes were satisfied by the *Universal Historical Bibliotheque* from 1687. New books were listed in the *Term Catalogues* – the forerunner of *Whitaker's Books in Print* and *The Bookseller* – for those too busy declaiming in the coffee house to browse in the bookshop.

For a while, coffee houses were the best place to go for books. In 1819, the British Museum acquired the book and pamphlet stock of three London coffee houses: Tom's in Devereux Court, George's in Temple Bar (both close to the Inns of Court) and the

Lloyd's Coffee house from a coloured aquatint by William Holland, 1798.

Bank coffee house in Threadneedle Street. This collection gives us a unique picture of the sort of books which were bought for the delectation of coffee house readers. From this, and from books from Tom's found in other libraries, we can be sure that Tom's had at least 135 books and pamphlets for the edification and education of its clientele. Most were political, military and religious, with some poetry, and translations from Tasso and Aristotle and a Milton translated into Latin. Lists of names in some of the Tom's books would suggest that the books could be borrowed. In the 1840s there may have been as many as 500 coffee house libraries providing this valuable public service well before the advent of public libraries.

Coffee shops, then, became the places of choice for conversation, debate and gossip amongst tradesman, politicians, journalists and lawyers, and one could even buy and sell shares and commodities. As the numbers of coffee houses proliferated they became more specialised, with different professions or with different interests congregating at a particular house. For example, booksellers and publishers met at the Chapter Coffee House in Paternoster Row – Charlotte and Anne Brontë were rare female visitors there when they arrived in London to resolve a problem with their publishers, Smith and Elder. Will's was the place for actors, or Wright's or the Bedford, all in Covent Garden; opera singers and dancing masters chorused in the Orange; lawyers adjudicated at Alice's and Hell Coffee House and artists canvassed at the Old Slaughter in St Martin's Lane. Up the road at the Rainbow and at Garraway's there were artists' clubs and exhibitions of prints. Child's Coffee House in St Paul's churchyard was where the clergy preached, as they did at St Paul's coffee house, also under the cathedral, visited once by Benjamin Franklin. Jonathan's in Exchange Alley had been the centre of 'jobbing', as the *Annual Register* of 1762 puts it; it 'had been a market, time out of mind, for buying and selling Government securities'. This came about because in 1697 the merchants had the stock-jobbers removed from the Royal Exchange, so they took their business dealings to the neighbouring coffee houses. It became the Stock Exchange in July 1773 and the brokers there 'christened the house with punch' according to the *Old and New London, Walter Thornbury 1883–1885*. Other financial industries, such as life assurance, general insurance and reinsurance, and investment banking, were all born in the coffee houses at this time. Officials of the East India Company, Hudson's Bay Company, and the African, Russian and Levant Companies met in coffee houses in the early days. Coffee houses occasionally witnessed slave trading. Like Edward Lloyd, many used their coffee house as a *poste restante;* the penny post had been established in 1680 and the ideal place to direct the mail was to the four or five hundred shops or coffee houses now often called 'penny post houses'.

As we have mentioned, the coffee house was the newspaper of the day, the internet indeed. Newspapers were distributed in the coffee houses; in the 1700s César-François de Saussure, the Swiss travel writer, remarked in *A Foreign View of England in the Reigns of George I and George II:*

> What attracts enormously in these coffee houses are the gazettes and other public papers. All Englishmen are great newsmongers. Workmen habitually begin the day by going to coffee rooms in order to read the latest news.

Runners would also be sent to go to the coffee houses with the latest 'news flash'. In Dublin, the many coffee houses were expected to have all the Irish papers as well as London editions. As in England, certain coffee houses hosted specific groups. Dick's was a second home to Tories and housed a printing press for Tory pamphlets and other party literature. A man named Lloyd was a printing proprietor who ran the Oxman Town coffee shop and then Lloyd's coffee shop. Dickson, the rival Whig, started his printing business in the back of Lloyd's first shop and went on to run four Whig coffee shops.

For one penny, customers bought a cup of coffee and admission, with access to newspapers and the opinions, advice and attitude of fellow patrons. The early coffee houses also served tea and chocolate but not alcohol; it is this that did much to foster an atmosphere in which it was possible to engage in more serious and nuanced conversation than was usually possible in the rowdy alehouse. The low admission price made them comparatively inclusive and in Oxford (and presumably Cambridge) they provided an exciting alternative to the exclusive and much more formal university lecture and tutorial.

The first Cambridge newspaper, the *Cambridge Journal and the Weekly Flying Post*, appeared on 22 September 1744. It was started by Robert Walker and Thomas James and printed 'next the Theatre Coffee House'.

However, the coffee house was by no means universally popular. Many hated the places – or affected to. In 1666 Pepys saw a play called *The Coffee-House*, and called it 'the most ridiculous, insipid play that ever I saw in my life'. The *coup de grâce*, however, is this excoriating fusillade describing the coffee house as:

> A lay-conventicle, good-fellowship turned puritan, ill-husbandry in masquerade; whither people come, after toping all day, to purchase, at the expense of their last penny, the repute of sober companions: a rota-room, that, like Noah's ark, receives

animals of every sort, from the precise diminutive band, to the hectoring cravat and cuffs in folio; a nursery for training up the smaller fry of virtuosi in confident tattling, or a cabal of kittling critics that have only learned to spit and mew... He, that comes often, saves two-pence a week in Gazettes, and has his news and his coffee for the same charge, as at a three-penny ordinary they give in broth to your chop of mutton; it is an exchange where haberdashers of political smallwares meet, and mutually abuse each other, and the public, with bottomless stories, and headless notions; the rendezvous of idle pamphlets, and persons more idly employed to read them; a high court of justice, where every little fellow in a camlet cloke takes upon him to transpose affairs both in church and state, to shew reasons against acts of parliament, and condemn the decrees of general councils.

The coffee house is hell on earth:

[It] stinks of tobacco worse than hell of brimstone; the coffee itself had the appearance of Pluto's diet-drink, that witches tipple out of dead men's skulls; and the company included a silly fop and a worshipful justice, a griping rook and a grave citizen, a worthy lawyer and an errant pickpocket, a reverend non-conformist and a canting mountebank, all blended together to compose an oglio of impertinence.

'Mad dog runs riot in coffee house'. Thomas Rowlandson (1757–1827), 1809. Note the reference to Cerberus – guard dog of Hades – on the sign. The scene is the chaos caused by a dog running riot through a coffee house. The dog stands on top of a table, knocking over the contents of a jug that spill over a man who has fallen from his seat and is lying on the floor. On the right, a bearded Jewish man looks up from his papers to where the commotion is while various gentlemen around the room attempt to eject the dog from the room using brooms, umbrellas and clubs. Others flee in terror.

But nothing could staunch the popularity of coffee and the coffee houses. In 1690 John Ray, the natural historian, remarked on coffee's ubiquity and expressed astonishment at the number of bushels being exported yearly from Arabia Felix, and was surprised that no other surrounding countries had yet jumped on the bandwagon.

By 1675, there were apparently more than 3,000 coffee houses in England alone. Some had bed and breakfast for overnight guests. Many seem to follow the same Turkish coffee house-type business model if their exotic names are anything to go by. We can only speculate on how many were actually run by Muslims or immigrants from the Levant. There were up to fifty-seven different 'Turk's Head' coffee houses; 'The Jerusalem Coffee-house'; various types of the 'Blackamoor' or 'Ye Blackmore's Head'; 'The Oriental Cigar Divan'; 'The Saracen's Head' (of Dickens fame); 'The Africa and Senegal Coffee-house'; 'The Sultaness'; 'The Sultan's Head'; 'Solyman's Coffee House'; and 'Morat Ye Great'; there is also the first Indian restaurant in London, 'The Hindoostanee' of 1810.

Some diversified with tobacco and hookah pipes, and tea and chocolate were also served. The serving staff often seems to have dressed the part, and a 'black boy' was sometimes employed as a star attraction for customers. The signs outside, and the coffee tokens that were used to purchase inside, were often exotically turbaned. Somewhat later, Hogarth's portrait of himself has him wearing a turban, which is decidedly ironic in view of his opinions about coffee. It seems, in fact, that turban-wearing became à la mode for coffee house clientele generally.

The 'Great Turk Coffee House' (also known as 'Morat Ye Great' above) in Exchange Alley in 1662 was famous for its bust of Sultan Almurath IV himself, 'the most detestable tyrant that ever ruled the Ottoman Empire'. The customer could buy coffee, tea and tobacco here, as well as chocolate and a range of sherbets, which, in the words of the *Mercurius Publicus* (12–19 March 1662), were 'made in Turkie; made of lemons, roses, and violets perfumed'. Tea was first added to a price list at Thomas Garraway's Sultans' Head Coffee House in Change Alley, in 1657. Garraway had some selling to do to clear his stocks of this mysterious new beverage so he promoted it through a distribution of pamphlets and an advertisement in *Mercurius Politicus* on 30 September 1658, the first advertisement for a commodity in a London newspaper. It read:

> That Excellent, and by all Physicians approved, China drink, called by the Chinese, Tcha, by other nations Tay alias Tee,…sold at the Sultaness-head, ye Cophee-house in Sweetings-Rents, by the Royal Exchange, London.

White's, the Cocoa Tree and St James' were essentially chocolate or cocoa houses, but, no doubt, a cup of coffee could be had in each; they were of the same character as coffee houses and gave off the same literary, social and commercial atmosphere. In April 1773 a fire destroyed White's Chocolate House, which reopened as White's Club, the first of many London houses to become an exclusive gentleman's club. The Cocoa Tree was the haunt of Tories, Arthur's that of Whigs.

The Sultaness Coffee House was mentioned by Dickens in a number of his works, notably *Little Dorrit*, implying that this particular coffee-house survived for about 200 years.

Garraway's just before demolition.

The memorial plaque at 32 Cornhill is all that is left of Garraway's. It reads: 'Garraway's Coffee House, a place of great commercial transaction and frequented by people of quality.' According to the barber Thomas Rugg, writing in his *Diurnal*, 'Coffee, chocolate and a kind of drink called *tee*' were 'sold in almost every street in 1659'.

The famous Grecian Coffee House was first established in about 1665 at Wapping Old Stairs by a Greek sailor called George Constantine. The enterprise was a resounding success and by 1677 Constantine could afford to move to more salubrious premises in Devereux Court, off Fleet Street. In the 1690s the Grecian was the favoured meeting place of the Whigs, the opposition party at the time. Soon it was to become a haunt of members of the Royal Society, including Sir Isaac Newton, Sir Hans Sloane, Edmund Halley and the poet and politician Joseph Addison. Isaac Newton once dissected a dolphin on the table there. Classics scholars were frequent patrons and on one occasion amused themselves by trying to arrange the events of the *Iliad* into chronological order. Another time, two friends among them fought a duel in the street outside because they could not agree on where to put the accent on a Greek word. The loser was run through with a sword and died there and then. By 1803, however, the Grecian was overtaken by lawyers and it finally closed in 1843 to become the Devereux Public House, host to many a Freemasonry Meeting, and Oliver Goldsmith's local. The Grecian was the favourite coffee house of famous Shakespearean scholar Edmond Malone. In April 1776 he captured the ambience there when he wrote his father a letter saying, 'I am at present writing in a coffee-house, in the midst of so much noise and bustle—the celebrated anti-Sejanus (Mr. Scott) on one

The Grecian in Devereux Court off the Strand with the bust of Samuel Johnson on the façade, as depicted in an issue of *Look & Learn.*

side and Mr. [Charles] Macklin [the actor] on the other—that I can't add anything more at present.'

The London coffee house saw its zenith in the eighteenth century, with commentaries on all aspects of life recorded by Addison in the *Spectator,* Steele in the *Tatler* and Mackay in *Journey Through England* in 1724. Literary soirées and coteries held at the Turk's Head in the Strand from 1763 to 1783 involved such eminences as Samuel Johnson, his biographer Boswell, Oliver Goldsmith, the actor David Garrick, Edmund Burke, the artist Sir Joshua Reynolds, historian Edward Gibbon and economist Adam Smith.

Lord Macaulay gives a vivid and important history of coffee-house life from its earliest days in his mid-nineteenth century *History of England*:

> The coffee house must not be dismissed with a cursory mention. It might indeed at that time have been not improperly called a most important political institution. No Parliament had sat for years…Nothing resembling the modern newspaper existed. In such circumstances the coffee-houses were the chief organs through which the public opinion of the metropolis vented itself …

The coffee house was a place of social and political consequence, a third chamber of government; the one you went to defined you:

> The convenience of being able to make appointments in any part of the town, and of being able to pass evenings socially at a very small charge, was so great that the fashion spread fast … Every coffee-house had one or more orators to whose

eloquence the crowd listened with admiration, and who soon became what the journalists of our time have been called, a Fourth Estate of the realm… Foreigners remarked that the coffee-house was that which especially distinguished London from all other cities; that the coffee-house was the Londoner's home, and that those who wished to find a gentleman commonly asked, not whether he lived in Fleet Street or Chancery Lane, but whether he frequented the Grecian or the Rainbow.

The coffee house was, up to a point only, socially inclusive; women and servants were excluded so at least 70 per cent of the population had no business there. Nevertheless, it was the home of all serious literary discussion, a common room for the medical profession:

> Nobody was excluded from these places who laid down his penny at the bar … Nowhere was the smoking more constant than at Will's … One group debated whether 'Paradise Lost' ought not to have been in rhyme. There were … sheepish lads from the universities, translators and index-makers in ragged coats of frieze. The great press was to get near the chair where John Dryden sat … To bow to the Laureate, and to hear his opinion of Racine's last tragedy … was thought a privilege. A pinch from his snuff-box was an honour sufficient to turn the head of a young enthusiast. There were coffee-houses where the first medical men might be consulted. Dr. John Radcliffe, who in the year 1685 rose to the largest practice in London, came daily … to Garraway's; and was to be found, surrounded by surgeons and apothecaries, at a particular table.

Many physicians frequented Batson's coffee house – a veritable consulting house in the days before doctors did ward rounds in hospitals. In time, people would make a special visit and pay to hear a series of lectures at a coffee house or attend a pre-arranged debate; the coffee houses came to be known as 'penny universities' because people could go to them to further their knowledge. The coffee house became an early form of adult education, or night school.

They were also a haunt for Puritans, Jews and Papists alike:

> There were Puritan coffee-houses where no oath was heard … Jew coffee-houses where dark eyed money-changers from Venice and Amsterdam greeted each other; and Popish coffee-houses where, as good Protestants believed, Jesuits planned over their cups another great fire, and cast silver bullets to shoot the King.

Garraway's in Change Alley is the source of a story that would have it that, when a celebrated actor was cast for the part of Shylock, he made daily visits to the coffee houses near the Exchange that 'by a frequent intercourse and conversation with the unforeskin'd race' he might learn how to act just like them.

Like it or not, coffee was by now well established, its consumption *de riguer*. 'And now, alas! The drink has credit got, And he's no gentleman who drinks it not,' moans Walter Thornbury in *Old and New London* (1883–1885).

Coffee could be had at the nineteenth-century tea gardens at the spa that was Bagnigge Wells near present-day King's Cross; 'ladies and gentlemen may depend on having the best of Tea, Coffee, etc'. In the twentieth century, Lockharts ran fifty coffee rooms in Liverpool and London, while the Express Dairy and Kardomah both had their own establishments.

But coffee was not just about cosmopolitan London or academic Oxford. What we see proliferating in the commercial capital and among the dreaming spires was replicated, naturally on a smaller scale, throughout the kingdom. In York, for example, coffee houses were legion. The rise of the coffee house coincided with a flood of books, pamphlets and newspapers that facilitated the transmission of political argument and made it more accessible than ever before. Charles II, seeing that that the printed word could be as much an ally as an enemy, passed 'An Act for Preventing the frequent Abuses in Printing Seditious, Treasonable, and Unlicensed Books and Pamphlets; and for the Regulating of Printing and Printing.' The Act – better known as the Printing or Licensing Act – passed into law on 10 June 1662, restricting printing to a limited number of presses, mostly in London. Apart from Oxford, Cambridge and York, printing was outlawed in provincial England until the Act was allowed to lapse in 1695, freeing printers to set up presses in provincial towns. Nowhere exemplifies better the link between the coffee house and printing and publishing than the city of York, where one fed the other.

There was a plethora of coffee houses in York from 1669. At least thirty are recorded, among which were Parker's in Minster Yard next to a bowling alley; the Garrick in Low

The inextricable link between the early coffee houses with printing and publishing can be seen at Coffee Yard, the home of a number of coffee houses and the printer's devil scowling down round the corner in Stonegate – an area of York with a long history of publishing, printing and bookselling that is now sadly gone.

Petergate; Wombwell and Wink's, Harrison's in Petergate and later Nessgate; Iveson's, also in Petergate, Duke's near to the Ouse Bridge; and Brigg's on the corner of Stonegate and Coffee Yard – as well as William Tuke's Roasting House. As one of thirty-one York tea dealers in 1823 and importers of tea, coffee and chocolate, the Tukes were the exclusive holders in the north of England of a licence that permitted the processing of coffee beans and the sale of roasted coffee, and of tea and chocolate. Chicory was grown around York for a time in the nineteenth century and sold to merchants who sold it on as an additive to coffee. The 'Printer's Devil' effigy at 33 Stonegate at the corner of Coffee Yard has been glaring down on us since the 1880s and signifies the importance and prevalence of the printing, bookselling and publishing industries in the area. A printer's devil was a printer's apprentice, a factotum. Printing was commonly known as 'the black art' on account of the inks. Coffee, of course, is popularly known as the devil's drink. John Glaisby's bookshop and library was in Coney Street; in 1848 it had been the premises of William Hargrove's *York Herald*, next to the George Hotel and known then as Kidd's Coffee House.

Coffee was indirectly responsible for York becoming a major chocolate manufacturing city. Mary Tuke ran her original grocery business in the city, and was joined by her nephew William in 1746 as an apprentice; he inherited the business on her death in 1752 and became a freeman grocer and member of the Merchant Adventurers. The shop specialised in the sale of coffee, chicory and drinking chocolate; brands such Tukes' Rich Cocoa, Tukes' Plain Chocolate, British Cocoa Coffee and Tukes' Milk Chocolate were brought to market. It was this tea and

Coffee was one of the key weapons in the Temperance wars. This photo shows a Temperance coffee cart outside York railway works offering an alternative to railway workers to the swift pint at lunchtimes. The Rowntrees were key players in this battle against beer.

coffee business that Henry Rowntree bought in 1862 and from which the Rowntree chocolate business grew.

John White was the Stonegate printer 'over against the Star', and the only one in the country brave enough to take on the printing of William of Orange's manifesto after his landing at Torbay in 1688. White was imprisoned at Hull for his troubles until the city surrendered to William. The king promptly rewarded him with a warrant appointing him 'Their Majesties' Printer for the City of York and the Five Northern Counties'. In 1718, his widow, Grace, became the first woman to establish a newspaper in York, the *York Mercury*, in Coffee Yard.

In 1818 the York Arms in High Petergate was the Chapter Coffee House, then the Eclipse and then became the Board after an 1838 rebuild. In 1843 it reverted to the Chapter Coffee House in 1843 and finally became the York Arms again in 1860. The Ancient Society of York Florists was established in 1768 and is the world's oldest horticultural society, originally in Colliergate and at Baynes Coffee House in Petergate. The eccentric Thomas Gent (d. 1778) published scores of chap books from his publishing house in Coffee Yard. In 1841 a Temperance Coffee House had opened in Colliergate, changing its name to the Commercial Temperance Hotel on its move to Low Ousegate in 1843. In the early 1890s there was a Temperance Society coffee stand in Queen Street dissuading railway workers from mixing work with alcoholic drink.

Today, York is the home of a multitude of coffee-cum-tea shops, perhaps the most famous of which are the two Bettys in the city.

A busy day in the St Helen's Square Bettys in 1988. (Courtesy of *York Press*)

The popularity of coffee owes much to tea and chocolate. Thomas Twining purchased Tom's Coffee House at 216 The Strand in 1706 and set up his tea empire; in 1824 John Cadbury opened his tea, coffee and cocoa shop in Bull Street, Birmingham, after completing apprenticeships first at John Cudworth's grocers in Leeds, then in London at the East India Company's bonded warehouse and then at the Sanderson, Fox and Company teahouse. In York, Joseph Rowntree Snr laid down the law for apprentices in their shop in Pavement:

> Be explicit in stating the particular kind of article wanted: e.g. if Coffee is ordered, state on order, whether whole, ground, mixed or genuine is wanted – if Tea – Black, Mixed, Assam, or whole-leaf: if Sugar, Lump, Raw or Moist.

In 1754 Robert Bartholomew advertised his White Conduit House tavern-cum-pleasure garden with the following copy:

> I have completed a long walk, with a handsome circular fish-pond, a number of shady pleasant arbours, enclosed with a fence seven feet high to prevent being the least incommoded from people in the fields; hot loaves and butter every day, milk directly from the cows, coffee, tea, and all manner of liquors in the greatest perfection.

Charles Edward Taylor, a Quaker, and son of a York master grocer, set his business with 'Kiosk' tea and coffee shops in fashionable Harrogate at 11 Parliament Street and

Taylor's coffee house in York's Stonegate. Today, it houses a second Bettys in the city. The card is published by Colin Baxter Photography.

Bettys Dive. On 1 February 1945 J. E. McDonald was the first of 600 airmen to scratch their names on the mirror at Bettys during the Second World War. Also known as Bettys Bar it was a regular haunt of the hundreds of airmen stationed in and around York; these included many Canadians from Number 6 Bomber Group. One signatory, Jim Rogers, borrowed a waitress' diamond ring to scratch his name on the mirror. Many have returned to reflect on their efforts. The mirror is still on display downstairs in Bettys but many of the signatories did not survive the war. The photo, courtesy of *York Press*, shows Pam Broadbent giving it a good clean.

Ilkley after an apprenticeship at James Ashby, the London tea dealers. The kiosks were followed by Café Imperials in both towns: Ilkley opened in 1896; the Harrogate branch in 1907, in the mock baronial castle now occupied by Bettys. The Ilkley Bettys is the old Taylor's 'Kiosk' Café and Bettys Stonegate York occupies the former Taylors 'Kiosk' café.

Thomas Twining typifies the paradox of tea and coffee houses. Twining took over Tom's Coffee House in Devereux Court, Fleet Street, in 1706 and set about developing his tea business from the shop next door, at the sign of the Golden Lyon, from where he sold tea to other coffee houses including Button's in Covent Garden. Between 1716 and 1722, Button bought packets of coffee every day, along with other groceries such as Bohea tea, chocolate, sugar, snuff and rum. His coffee cost him between 5s 6d and 6s 8d per pound while his tea set him back between 16s and 18s per pound. Coffee purchases were four times that of tea, but the volume suggests that tea was an increasingly popular choice of beverage in his coffee house, despite the higher price. The image of the two drinks, nevertheless, remained quite distinct. Coffee was still a man's drink, consumed in the coffee house among like-minded men, and women were barred from coffee houses. Tea remained a wealthy woman's drink, drunk in the home by women and bought by women at places such as Twinings.

Disorder of one sort or another – be it prostitution at Moll King's, brawling or highwaymen conspiring to waylay well-heeled guests – led coffee houses and chocolate houses such as St. James and the Cocoa-Tree, to follow White's into a private membership business model. This would pave the way for the demise of the coffee shop and its culture. The fashion for and huge popularity of tea impacted too and it was not long before Britain and Ireland became nations of tea lovers and tea drinkers – a fashion which Charles II's queen, Catherine of Braganza, ignited when she brought cases of tea with her from Portugal as part of her dowry, which also included the port of Bombay, in 1662. Tea consumption in England rose from 800,000 lb per annum in 1710 to 100 million lb per annum in 1721; from a practical point of view, making a cup of tea was a lot easier and quicker than making a cup of coffee.

Woman, unless prostitutes haunting some of the later, less salubrious houses, were excluded and they let their resentment be known:

> A coffee house habitué is someone who lodges at home, but he lives at the coffee-house. He converses more with newspapers, gazettes and votes, than with his shop-books, and his constant application to the publick takes him off all care for his private home. He is always settling the nation, yet could never manage his own family.

So said Mary Astell, in *An Essay in Defence of the Female Sex* in 1696. Astell was merely chiming with all the wives left at home with their cups of tea who seem to have been concerned about much more than just male fecklessness; in 1674 there had been the vitriolic 'The Women's Petition Against Coffee' in which wives complained that their husbands were forever absent from the home and family, neglecting their domestic duties, 'turning Turk', and all for 'a little base, black, thick, nasty, bitter, stinking nauseous puddle water'. Coffee 'made men as unfruitful as the deserts whence that unhappy berry is said to be brought: that the offspring of our mighty ancestors would dwindle into a succession of apes and pigmies'. To some, seventeenth-century erectile dysfunction was brought on by this noxious puddle. But to no avail; the 'coffee politicians' just ignored them – erection or no erection – and by the start of the eighteenth century there were at least 550 coffee houses going strong. In 1663 *The Maiden's Complaint Against Coffee* pamphlet was published. However, men did not take this criticism lying down and *Men's Answer to the Women's Petition Against Coffee* was the retort. It protested that it was 'base adulterate wine' and 'muddy ale' that made men impotent. Coffee, on the other hand, was the Viagra of the day, making 'the erection more vigorous, the ejaculation more full, add[ing] a spiritual ascendency to the sperm'. Pfizer could never have found a better opinion leader.

Some historians believe that women did go into coffee houses, but, because of the frenzied hubbub usually to be found there and the politics and commerce being discussed, they never entered in great numbers or made a habit of going in. There is, however, evidence of women conducting business in coffee houses (in Bath, for example), gambling and attending coffee house auctions; female news hawkers and female proprietors of coffeehouses; Anne Rochford and Moll King were among these 'coffee-women'.

Coffee, then, was a man's drink. Tea was for women. From the start, tea seems to have been associated with women. In Richard Ames's satire, *The Bacchanalian Sessions: Or the Contention of Liquors* published in 1693, tea loses out to coffee and other coffee house drinks due to its frivolous nature; Ames describes it as 'a drink much admir'd by the Ladies'. Courtesans were said to prefer it, due probably to its expense and its luxurious image. In 1702 Queen Anne's poet laureate, Nahum Tate, composed his thirty-six page *Panacea: A Poem upon Tea*, which describes in no small detail the discovery and production of tea – a subject of 'delicacy' and 'decency' perfect as an 'Entertainment for the Ladies'. Duncan Campbell wrote his *A Poem Upon Tea* in 1735, also dedicated to women; here he describes how 'when at Tea they sit' women are 'soberly inclin'd' and 'to one another affable and kind'. Indeed, 'Tea is the School at which they learn their Wit'; the preface asks of 'The Masculine Reader' what he would do 'without some female love and Tea'. Tea then represents womanliness and domesticity; the serving of tea in the home was the female equivalent to male socialisation outdoors in the coffee house. 'Tea is indeed the Tobacco of women', claimed George Poore, 1883.

Many coffee houses were eccentric and individualistic. For example, the walls of Don Saltero's Chelsea coffeehouse were exotically adorned with stuffed birds and animals; at Lunt's in Clerkenwell Green, patrons could sip coffee and have a haircut by owner John Gale Jones; at John Hogarth's Latin Coffeehouse, also in Clerkenwell, patrons were encouraged to speak in Latin at all times; there was even a floating coffeehouse, the Folly of the Thames, moored outside Somerset House, where dancing went on until the early hours.

There was nothing remotely Spanish about Don Saltero – he was really just plain James Salter. Coffee apart, Salter offered impromptu dental extractions, haircuts, fiddle-playing and set up a museum in his house. Steele describes it nicely:

The Folly moored on the Thames off Somerset House. The magistrates closed it down because it had become 'so common and notorious'.

When I came into the coffee-house ... I had not time to salute the company, before my eye was diverted by ten thousand gimcracks round the room, and on the ceiling. When my first astonishment was over, comes to me a sage of thin and meagre countenance; which, aspect made me doubt, whether reading or fretting had made it so philosophic: but I very soon perceived him to be of that sect which the ancients call Gingivistā; in our language, tooth-drawers. I immediately had a respect for the man; for these practical philosophers go upon a very rational hypothesis, not to cure, but to take away the part affected.

In Covent Garden, the Bedford Coffee house had a 'theatrical thermometer' with 'temperatures' on a scale from 'excellent' to 'execrable', a veritable trial by coffee for playwrights who must at times have dreaded walking into the place after the opening performance of their latest play. Politicians suffered the same ordeal in the Westminster coffee houses after delivering speeches to Parliament. The Hoxton Square coffee house was notorious for its mock insanity trials, where a suspected lunatic would be tied up and wheeled into the coffee room. A jury would examine, prod and interrogate the alleged madman and then vote on whether to imprison the accused in one of the local asylums. Among the coffee-houses of Covent Garden were the Bedford, King's, Rawthmell's and Tom's. The Bedford had among its patrons Fielding, Pope, Sheridan, Garrick, Horace Walpole and others. Its habitués, according to the Connoisseur, 'afforded a greater variety of nearly the same type as those to be found at George's'. The Bedford became 'the emporium of wit, the seat of criticism, and the standard of taste.' Oliver Goldsmith had his letters addressed to George's. The Bedford was where James Hackman murdered Martha Ray as she was leaving a Covent Garden theatre on the night of 17 April, 1779. Rawthmell's was posh and where the Society of Arts in was founded in 1754. Tom's took its name from the first landlord, Captain Thomas West, who, driven mad by the agony of gout, committed suicide by throwing himself from one of his own windows.

In 1712, the Starbucks site on Russell Street was Button's coffee house where, nailed to the wall, the white marble head of a lion with gaping jaws glowered. Patrons were invited to feed it with letters, limericks and stories; the best of the lion's meals were published in a weekly edition of Joseph Addison's Guardian newspaper, called 'The Roarings of the Lion':

Whatever the lion swallows I shall digest for the use of the public ... It will be set up in Button's coffee-house in Covent-garden, who is directed to shew the way to the lion's head, and to instruct young authors how to convey his works into the mouth of it with safety and secrecy.

Steele placed an advertisement for a course of lectures in Daniel Button's coffee house, which he helped establish: 'Beginning January 11, 1713–14, a course of philosophical lectures on mechanics, hydrostatics, pneumatics, optics ... This course of experiments is to be performed by Mr William Whiston and Francis Hauksbee.'

Whiston, however, had a reputation for digressing from his mathematics to make tedious religious sermons. Henry Newman wrote a letter to Richard Steele on 10 August 1713: 'to conjure him silence upon all topics foreign to the mathematics in his conversation or lectures at your coffee house. He has an itch to be venting his notions about baptism and the Arian doctrine but your authority can restrain him'.

Another regular customer of Button's was John Arbuthnot, writer of many popular pamphlets, often signing off with 'From a sparkish pamphleteer of Button's Coffee House'.

Mathematics in particular owes much to coffee houses and its patrons. There was a play by Thomas Sydserf called *Tarugo's Wiles, or, The Coffee House. A Comedy*. In Act 3 there is a mathematics-inspired conversation between two coffee house customers.

Slaughter's Coffee House in St Martin's Lane opened in 1692. It was famous for its chess players and as a place for those seeking mathematical advice. Abraham de Moivre, friend of Newton and Leibniz, was the resident mathematician at Slaughter's; he cut a rather pathetic figure and would give advice on risk, or chance of loss to make a little money; he also played chess for money. John Harris, who graduated from Oxford University in 1686, wrote: 'Lectures were here read in experimental philosophy and chemistry and a very tolerable course of mathematics taught, then [I was given] leave to teach mathematics'. Harris gave a mathematics and astronomy lecture course at the Marine Coffee House in Birchin Lane every year between 1698 and 1704. He even produced a book, the textbook to accompany his course, which he published in 1703 called *Description and Uses of the Celestial and Terrestrial Globes and of Collins' Pocket Quadrant*.

In Charing Cross there was the Cannon; the coffee-house run by Alexander Man, and known, unsurprisingly, as Man's. Man was appointed coffee, tea, and chocolate-maker to William III, which allowed his establishment to be described as the Royal Coffee House. It had a third name, Old Man's Coffee-house, to distinguish it from the Young Man's on the other side of the street. The British Coffee House was in Cockspur Street; members included Spankie, Dr Haslam, author of several works on insanity.

Politics and literature were most often on the agenda at the Smyrna coffee house on the north side of Pall Mall. An early edition of the Tatler describes 'that cluster of wise heads':

> to all ingenious gentlemen in and about the cities of London and Westminster, who have a mind to be instructed in the noble sciences of music, poetry, and politics, that they repair to the Smyrna coffee-house in Pall-mall, betwixt the hours of eight and ten at night, where they may be instructed gratis, with elaborate essays, by word of mouth on all or any of the above-mentioned arts. The disciples are to prepare their bodies with three dishes of bohea, and purge their brains with two pinches of snuff.

The Hindoostanee Coffee House of 1810 was not really a coffee house but rather London's first curry house. It was set up by a Sake Dean Mahomet who arrived here from Bengal via Ireland, eloped with and married his Irish wife, and opened his ornate coffee-house-cum-Indian restaurant at 34 George Street, off Portman Square. The restaurant offered Hookha 'with real Chilm tobacco, and Indian dishes ... allowed by the greatest epicures to be unequalled to any curries ever made in England.' Unfortunately, the business failed. He then moved on to Brighton to establish a highly successful and England's first Indian Vapour Baths and Shampooing Establishment where the Queen's

WEST COUNTRY MAILS AT THE GLOUCESTER COFFEE HOUSE, PICCADILLY.

West Country mails at the Gloucester coffee house in 1828 in Piccadilly. Coloured aquatint after a painting by James Pollard engraved by C. Rosenberg. Published by Thomas McLean, London and Paris, 1828.

Hotel now stands, and soon after became King George IV's 'shampooing surgeon'. Back then, 'shampooing' was an Indian massage; the word 'shampooing' did not take on its modern meaning of washing the hair until the 1860s. He was the first Asian to write a book in English, the 1794 *The Travels of Dean Mahomet*.

There were coffee houses, and there were coffee houses. In the mid-eighteenth century, Tom King's Coffee House was a notorious establishment in Covent Garden, operating until dawn each night as nothing less than a thinly disguised brothel. The key to its survival was the absence of beds: without beds King could swerve round any charges of keeping a bawdy house, an offence that could attract a whipping and a prison sentence.

Tom came from good stock: he was born in 1694 to Thomas King, a squire from Thurlow, Essex, and Elizabeth Cordell, the daughter of a baronet, Sir John Cordell. He was educated at Eton and King's College, Cambridge. Around 1720, after a short-lived marriage, he and his second wife Moll reunited after a break-up, and opened a coffee house in one of the shacks in Covent Garden, which was rented from the Duke of Bedford at £12 a year. She was a lowly market girl. Also known as Elizabeth Adkins, Mary or Maria Godson, Moll was a prostitute, pickpocket and thief. She may even have been the protagonist in Daniel Defoe's *Moll Flanders*.

The Kings' coffee house was a spectacular success, with the owners' connections at both ends of the social spectrum, all united by that universal common denominator – sex. A second and third shack followed, as did the added attraction of the pretty black

The inscrutable Moll King.

barmaid, Black Betty (also known as Tawny Betty). One of the slogans for Tom King's Coffee House was the place where anybody could find a willing partner, open to "all gentlemen to whom beds were unknown". Over time Hogarth, Alexander Pope, John Gay, and Henry Fielding were all clients. Fielding mentions it in both *The Covent Garden Tragedy and Pasquin,* and Tobias Smollett in *The Adventures of Roderick Random.*

It was not just men in search of sex (and coffee?) who were attracted to Tom King's. That fervent moral campaigner Sir John Gonson of the Society for the Reformation of Manners, and inveterate brothel raider, regularly sent incognito informers in to try and uncover illegalities. To counter this, Tom and Moll developed their own secret language, 'Talking Flash' (similar to thieves' cant or rogues' cant, or peddler's French – a far cry from the polite and urbane conversation of Steele or Addison), to render their conversations quite incomprehensible to outsiders.

On Tom's death, the coffee house became known as Moll King's Coffee House and business continued much as before. Moll, however, took to drinking the alcoholic stock and the establishment's reputation for violence, corruption and disorder grew. That did not, however, deter the patronage of fashionable society; one night George II paid a visit and was challenged to a fight for ogling the companion of one of the men next to him, thus occasioning a hasty regal exit. After a spell in prison for riotous behaviour and refusing to pay a £200 fine, Moll ran the coffee house until around 1745, when she retired to live in her villa at decidedly up-market Haverstock Hill. She died on 17 September 1747, leaving a fortune.

Carpenter's Coffee House (later known as 'The Finish', 'The Queen's Head' and 'Jack's') was a coffee house of similar ilk and reputation, also in Covent Garden; it was established by George Carpenter around 1762. As with King's, coffee was low down on the price list. The quality of their coffee was decidedly poor. In 1766 William Hickey, a

A scene of turmoil in a coffee house near the Olympic Theatre on Wych Street – although it could just as easily be Moll's.

lawyer and author, described it as: 'a Spartan mixture difficult to ascertain the ingredients but which was served as coffee'. Beer and punch were also served. By 1768 Carpenter's was known by the nickname 'The Finish', describing its terminal (in both senses of the word at times) role for those out for a night on the town; when all else was shut, there was always Carpenter's.

Carpenter died around 1785, so from 1788 it was run by Elizabeth Butler, a former brothel-keeper, who had run a successful business in King Street nearby. The reputation deteriorated yet further; it was a place where thieves and murderers would lie in wait for their victims. At the beginning of the nineteenth century it had become a favourite haunt of boxers. A far cry indeed from the glittering literati in other coffee houses.

Coffee houses of all complexions – salubrious and salacious alike – were nevertheless still all the rage. The more civilised were not just convivial and useful places to meet for artists and writers but business and banking transactions took place in them; Freemasons had their Lodge meetings in them. It was said that in a coffee house a man could 'pick up more useful knowledge than by applying himself to his books for a whole month'. Many coffee houses, due to their sea-born connections, even set up a postal system for collecting and carrying letters abroad. Often they had commercial links with Turkish baths, which were also enjoying a surge in popularity. They retained their reputation for being meeting places for religious or political dissidents and in the late seventeenth century were 'under suspicion as being centres of intrigue and treasonable-talk'.

The increasing sales of non-alcoholic beverages in the burgeoning coffee houses had serious economic implications for the Exchequer and for farmers. Farmers saw tea, coffee and brandy as unwelcome competition for their wheat, barley and malt – constituents of beer – and wanted them banned. In the 3,000 or so coffee houses allegedly operating in 1675, coffee was ordered in preference to the traditional glass of ale or gin – alcoholic beverages from which the Government received substantial tax revenues. Pascal Rosée alone sold over 600 dishes of coffee a day at the very dawn of the coffee revolution. Something had to be done to restore the shortfall in beer and gin consumption. Coffee was seen as an antidote to the commonplace drunkenness, violence and lust, providing a catalyst for civilised thought, sophistication and wit. For some, the temptation to compare the hedonism it erased with recent pre-Restoration Puritan austerity must have been irresistible. Rosée had triggered a coffee house sensation and his 'bitter Mohammedan gruel' was changing London life forever. As noted previously, in 1672 Charles II issued his Proclamation to restrain the spreading of false news, and licentious talking of matters of State and Government. Coffee houses were seen by the state as 'nurseries of sedition' and the public was urged to report any such anti-government scandal-mongering. They were looked upon with suspicion, especially by Royalists and Tories, fearful of a return to Civil War. According to the socially conservative lawyer and biographer Roger North, they were 'places of promiscuous resort' where 'gentlemen, citizens and underlings mingled' – a potentially explosive combination. Charles II saw them as centres of the 'most seditious, indecent and scandalous discourses'. He banned coffee houses from receiving any newspapers apart from the official London Gazette. Coffee houses seemed to have escaped the strictures of Cromwell's Puritanism but were, ironically, assaulted during the comparative liberalism in Charles' reign.

Nothing much changed, so in 1674 a similar proclamation was published, and another, more punitive still, at the end of 1675: *A proclamation for the suppression of coffee houses*. How far this was really done for commercial reasons or for genuine concern over simmering revolution we can only speculate. It is worth remembering, though, that the Popish Plot and the hysteria it caused from 1678 to 1681 was not far off. No doubt Charles' spies were good customers of the coffee houses, eavesdropping, stoking paranoia and inciting suspected enemies of the state in the verbal rough and tumble and indiscretions so commonly found there. Impossible to police and in the face of public disapproval, the proclamation was rescinded within eleven short days. Coffee and coffee houses, unlike the Stuarts, had come to stay. In 1676 the poet Andrew Marvell scorned Charles in his Dialogue between Two Horses:

> Though tyrants make laws, which they strictly proclaim,
> To conceal their own faults and to cover their shame…
> Let the city drink coffee and quietly groan, -
> They who conquered the father won't be slaves to the son.
> For wine and strong drink make tumults increase,
> Chocolate, tea, and coffee, are liquors of peace;
> No quarrels, or oaths are among those who drink'em
> 'Tis Bacchus and the brewer swear, damn'em! And sink'em!
> Then Charles thy edict against coffee recall,
> There's ten times more treason in brandy and ale.

Intellectuals, charlatans and scientists also used coffee houses to launch their latest projects and release 'leaks' to the press; and the sea-born trading companies such as the East India Company, the African Company and the Levant Company all made use of coffee houses, often to store their records. Newspapers, journals and pamphlets, as we have seen, were circulated with gusto and many of the literati wrote about coffee houses, and about those foreign 'moors' generally – write but what you know. Here is one anonymous piece from 1665 entitled 'The Character of a Coffee-House'.

> And if you see the great Morat
> With shash on's head instead of hat,
> Or any Sultan in his dress,
> Or picture of a Sultaness,
> Or John's admired curl'd pate,
> Or th' great Mogul in's Chair of State,
> Or Constantine the Grecian,
> Who 14 years was th' only man
> That made coffee for th' great Bashaw,
> Although the man he never saw;
> Of if you see a coffee-cup
> Filled from a Turkish pot, hung up
> Withing the clouds, and round it Pipes,
> Wax candles, stoppers, these are types
> And certain signs (with many more
> Would be too long to write them ore'),
> Which plainly do spectators tell
> That in that house they coffee sell.

As noted above, Turkish things became fashionable, helped no end by coffee and coffee houses with their exotic ambience, and were embraced by coffee house customers. Clothing suggestive of the Islamic world elided into the higher echelons of British society, particularly in cosmopolitan London. Another anonymous writer, 'W. P.', wrote, 'The English imitate all other people in their ridiculous Fashions … [and] with the Barbarous Indian he smoaks Tobacco. With the Turk he drinks Coffee.'

Ned Ward, in his journal the London Spy, may well have captured the essence and exotica of the London coffee house in his 1700 lampoon:

There was a rabble going hither and thither, reminding me of a swarm of rats in a ruinous cheese-store. Some came, others went; some were scribbling, others were talking; some were drinking [coffee], some smoking, and some arguing; the whole place stank of tobacco like the cabin of a barge. On the corner of a long table, close by the armchair, was lying a Bible. Beside it were earthenware pitchers, long clay pipes, a little fire on the hearth, and over it the high coffee pot. Beneath a small bookshelf, on which were bottles, cups, and an advertisement for a beautifier to improve the complexion, was hanging a parliamentary ordinance against drinking and the use of bad language. The walls were decorated with gilt frames, much as a smithy is decorated with horseshoes. In the frames were rarities; phials of a yellowish elixir, favourite pills and hair tonics, packets of snuff, tooth powder made from coffee grounds, caramels and cough lozenges. Had not my friend told me that he had brought me to a coffee-house, I would have regarded the place as the big booth of a cheap-jack.

Despite his satirical attack it did not take long for Ward himself to be seduced: 'When I had sat there for a while, and taken in my surroundings, I myself felt inclined for a cup of coffee.'

Attempts were made to maintain the high standing of coffee houses as places where politeness and refinement were highly regarded; just how successful they were, we cannot know. According to the first *Rules and Orders of the Coffee House*, published 1674, social equality was held in high esteem to such a degree that 'no man of any station need give his place to a finer man', suggesting that social status was ignored, as conversation was open to anyone regardless of class, rank, or political persuasion. Swearing was fined at one shilling; the instigator of a quarrel would have to purchase the offended party a cup of coffee. 'Maudlin lovers' were forbidden. 'Sacred things' were barred from coffee houses, as was criticising the state or the scriptures. Cards and dice were supposedly not allowed but wagers were limited to five shillings all the same. In some coffee houses any rules obviously fell on deaf ears …

So, how and why did it all come to an end? We know that from the end of the seventeenth century to the beginning of the eighteenth century, coffee houses were integral to the life of educated, business-minded upper and middle class men, particularly in London, Oxford, Cambridge and York. This was the golden age of the coffee shop, coinciding as it did with an explosion in organised commerce and the publication of domestic and foreign news. As the eighteenth century wore on, the private, members only, London club began to supplant the coffee shop. The state postal system, another fire at the Royal Exchange in 1838 and the establishment of Lloyd's in its own building led to coffee houses playing a much diminished role in British commercial and public life.

Most crucially, though, press censorship ended in 1695 and the print runs of newspapers mushroomed. Press censorship had been reasserted in 1662 with the Licensing Act, which controlled the content of all books, newspapers and pamphlets and restricted the number of newspaper publishers to twenty. The repeal of the Act meant that papers were now in ready supply and could be taken home to read; editorials and leaders did the job of the ad hoc coffee house discussion. You no longer had to go to the coffee shop to get your news feed. The freedom of the press, in every sense of the word, had been born.

By 1709 there were nineteen papers published in London with fifty-five editions per week. By 1760 over 150 different papers had come and gone. The thirty-five provincial papers had a joint circulation of 200,000 copies, substantial by the standards of the day. By 1833 the Manchester Coffee House & Newsroom (note the full name) took ninety-six papers every week plus periodicals and reviews; it cost 2*d* for entrance, papers and coffee. The nearby Exchange responded with ten papers, 186 on Saturday and a number of foreign papers. Tunbridge Wells had three coffee houses in 1739 – pens, paper and ink could be had for 5*s*. Morgan's was the place to go in Bath.

Magazines came along in the 1730s, further supplanting the role of the coffee shop with their blend of news digests, book reviews, advertisements, business information, announcements – everything the coffee shop had provided, but between two covers,

Musicians in Bettys, York, in 1979. (Courtesy of *York Press*)

and highly portable. The *Gentleman's Magazine*, first published in 1731, in London, is thought to have been the first general-interest magazine. The editor, Edward Cave, wrote under the pen name 'Sylvanus Urban'; he was the first to coin the word 'magazine', analogous to a military storehouse of varied materiel, derived from the Arabic makhazin 'storehouses'. The oldest consumer magazine still in print is the *Scots Magazine*, which was first published in 1739.

An adequate supply of newspapers, the birth of the magazine and the trend to take and read these at home sounded the death knell for the original brand of coffee house. They continued of course, but the social, commercial and academic urgency which had characterised them in the early days slowly diminished. The coffee house transformed, in some cases, into the exclusive and elitist gentlemen's clubs, some of which are still with us today, or else, in other cases, they might become the haunts of women of the night. Whatever, the days of the traditional coffee house were well and truly over by the mid-1700s.

4

Coffee Goes West and East

Captain John Smith, one of the founders of Virginia, introduced coffee to what was to become the United States of America when he brought coffee with him to Jamestown in 1607. Smith had become familiar with coffee from his travels in Turkey. It would seem that the Dutch West India Company declined to bring it to their first permanent settlement on Manhattan Island in 1624. Nor is there any record of coffee in the cargo of the *Mayflower* in 1620, although the vessel did include a wooden mortar and pestle, later used to make 'coffee powder'.

Coffee first appears in the records of the New England colony in 1670 as a beverage made from roasted beans, and sweetened with sugar or honey, and cinnamon. In 1683, the year following William Penn's settlement on the Delaware, he is buying coffee in the New York market paying 18s 9d pence per pound. According to Boston records, Dorothy Jones was the first to obtain a license to sell coffee and cuchaletto in 1670, the latter being a seventeenth century spelling of chocolate or cocoa.

As in England, coffee houses began to proliferate at the end of the seventeenth century. However, the distinction between early American coffee houses and alcohol-serving inns – where coffee was just another drink on the menu – is far from clear. America's first coffee house (or was it an inn?) opened in Boston in 1676, typical of the cities in which coffee, tea and beer were often served together in establishments which doubled as coffee houses and taverns. The London was probably the first coffee house to open; we learn from Samuel Gardner Drake in his *History and Antiquities of the City of Boston*, published in 1854, that 'Benj. Harris sold books there in 1689'. The Gutteridge was the second, followed by the British. As in London, coffee and commerce formed a genial and mutually beneficial partnership. The patrons of the Tontine coffee house were instrumental in the formation of the New York Stock Exchange and the City Tavern, or Merchants Coffee House, in Philadelphia was a venue for political leaders such as Washington, Jefferson and Hamilton.

The Green Dragon was where John Adams, James Otis and Paul Revere met as a 'ways and means committee' to secure freedom for the American colonies. This was the 'headquarters of the Revolution'. America was mostly a tea-drinking country until the Boston Tea Party incident of 1773, after which many colonists rejected coffee in favour of tea as a patriotic duty. Boston led to coffee being crowned 'king of the American

A Boston poster promoting coffee from around 1862 with U.S. sailor, two Zouaves, a soldier, and an eagle over US flags. Lithographer: A. Holland. Zouaves was the name for light infantry regiments in the French Army, normally serving in French North Africa between 1831 and 1962.

breakfast table', and the sovereign drink of the American people. Members of the Grand Lodge of Masons held their meetings in coffee houses.

If the patriots were ensconced in the Green Dragon, the loyalists were holed up at the British. It was here that James Otis was badly beaten up, after being lured there by political enemies. In 1750, some British redcoats staged the first theatrical entertainment given in Boston, playing Otway's *Orphan*. There, the first organisation of citizens to form a club set up the Merchants' Club in 1751. Members included officers of the king, colonial governors, army and navy leaders, and members of the Bar. As soon as the king's troops evacuated Boston, the name of the British was changed to the American. The nearby Bunch of Grapes was where the Declaration of Independence was famously read from the balcony in 1776.

The Boston coffee house reached its zenith in 1808, when the doors of the Exchange coffee house were thrown open. A veritable skyscraper of its day, it was built of stone, marble and brick, stood seven stories high, and cost $500,000. It was modelled on Lloyd's of London and was the hub of marine intelligence; its rooms ever thronged all day and evening with mariners, naval officers, marine and insurance brokers. The first floor was given over to trading, the next floor held a large dining room and on the other floors were living and sleeping rooms, of which there were more than 200. The Exchange was destroyed by fire in 1818 and later a successor was built.

Coffee had a slow start in New York, or New Amsterdam as it was first known. First records mention it about 1668; it replaced 'must', or beer, at the American breakfast table but had to compete with chocolate as well as tea. One very important characteristic of American coffee houses sets them apart from their European counterparts, and that is their use as a civic forum. Americans held court trials in the long, or assembly, room of the early coffee houses and often held their council meetings there. On the commercial front, the stock market made its headquarters in the Tontine coffee house in 1817, later to become the New York Stock and Exchange Board. The Merchants coffee house was home to an endless list of diverse organisations, including the Society of Arts; Knights of Corsica; Chamber of Commerce of the State of New York; Whig Society; Society of the New York Hospital; Society of the Sons of St. Patrick; Society for Promoting the Manumission of Slaves; Society for the Relief of Distressed Debtors; Black Friars Society; and Federal Republicans.

In Quaker Philadelphia Ye Coffee House, two London coffee houses, and the City tavern (also known as the Merchants coffee house) dominated the city's political and social life as meeting places for Quakers, ships' captains and merchants, who gathered to conduct their business. The second London coffee house was 'the pulsating heart of excitement, enterprise, and patriotism' of the early city. Leading citizens congregated there 'to sip their coffee from the hissing urn, and some of those stately visitors had their own stalls.' Carriages, horses, foodstuffs were sold there at auction. Philadelphians also sold slave men, women, and children, inhumanely exhibiting them on a platform in front of the coffee house.

Conrad Leonhard's coffee house in St Louis was famous for its coffee and coffee cake from 1844 to 1905. Two coffee houses in Chicago were the Washington coffee house

The British bark *Minmanueth* ran aground in 1873 on the south shore near Miacomet Pond in Nantucket. Spectators watched as 4,000 bags of coffee were offloaded to lighten the load before towing the ship to safety. (Free coffee for all! Courtesy of the Nantucket Historical Association, P6454, photo by Josiah Freeman)

MINMANUETH   NANTUCKET, M/

and the Exchange coffee house. In New Orleans, much of the business of the city was transacted in the coffee houses. The *brûleau* – coffee with orange juice, orange peel, and sugar, with cognac burned and mixed in it – originated in the New Orleans coffee house, and led to its gradual spread into the saloon bar.

In 1871 John Arbuckle invented a machine to fill, weigh, seal, and label paper packages of coffee. Arbuckle marketed his Arbuckle Ariosa coffee from his New York factory – the first mass-produced coffee product to be sold nationwide. Arbuckle went on to become the world's largest coffee importer as well as America's largest shipper, owning every South American merchant ship.

The New York Coffee Exchange was established in 1882. In 1886 Joel Cheek, a former grocer, named his coffee blend 'Maxwell House' after the Nashville hotel where it was the most popular blend. By the 1970s annual sales of instant coffee in the United States exceeded 200 million lb.

Coffee was introduced to Brazil in 1727, although it never really got off the ground until after independence in 1822 when huge tracts of rainforest were cleared for coffee plantations, first around Rio de Janeiro and later São Paulo.

The Brazilian coffee trade was reputedly ignited by a love affair. A Brazilian coastguard officer, Lieutenant Colonel Francisco de Melo Palheta, was sent to arbitrate a border dispute between the French and the Dutch colonies in Cayenne, French Guyana. The colonel enjoyed the coffee there. He also enjoyed the Governor's wife, who in turn loved him, and, at his request, said farewell to him with a bouquet in which she had hidden cuttings and fertile seeds of *arabica* coffee. These were subsequently grown back in Brazil, establishing the production that has dominated world trade for 200 years. By 1800, Brazil had become the largest producer of coffee in the world.

In 1938 the Nestlé Company developed freeze-dried Nescafé instant coffee at the request of the Brazilian government, who were anxious for ways to dispose of its coffee surplus. The coffee was marketed first to the public in Switzerland as a kind of consumer trial. Brazil issued the first coffee-scented postage stamp in 2002.

In 1723 Gabriel de Clieu, a French naval officer, introduced a coffee plant to the French territory of Martinique in the Caribbean after stealing a cutting from the king's coffee tree from the Jardin des Plantes, Paris. Fifty years later, there were an estimated 18 million coffee trees there. In the end, 90% of the world's *arabica* coffee came from this plant. Coffee was grown in Santo Domingo (now the Dominican Republic) from 1734, and by 1788 it was supplying half the world's coffee. Slavery on coffee plantations contributed to the Haitian Revolution. In 1730 the British took coffee to Jamaica. Guatemala got its first coffee crop in 1760; Costa Rica in 1779 and Mexico the following year. In 1825 Hawaii received coffee from Jesuits in Rio de Janeiro. Bourbon coffee seedlings arrived in South and Central America.

Columbia exported 500,000 bags of coffee in 1905. This doubled by 1915. In 1906 an English chemist working in Guatemala, George Constant Washington, noticed a powdery condensation forming on his silver coffee carafe spout. Washington soon created a process that is used to create the first mass-produced soluble coffee, or instant coffee. He called it calls Red-E Coffee and began selling it in 1909.

In 1887, coffee first arrived in Tonkin, Indo-China. In 1893 coffee plants from Brazil were brought to Tanganyika (present-day Tanzania) and Kenya where they were successfully cultivated. Coffee took off in Queensland, Australia in 1896.

5

Modern Coffee Culture

The preference for coffee over tea among our continental neighbours was clearly evident in the First World War. The 12,000 officers and 320,000 men of the Army Service Corps (equal to the size of the entire British army originally sent over to France and Belgium) had the awesome task of catering for the 5 million British troops, 3 million on the Western Front alone, on a daily basis. In 1914 the daily ration included 5/8 of an ounce of tea; other beverages issued were 1/10 of a gill of lime juice (where fresh vegetables were not issued) and half a gill of rum at the discretion of the battalion commander; some of these officers were teetotal and prohibited their men from having any. The Germans, on

Some of the many types of coffee. From a postcard designed by Martin Wiscombe and published by J. Salmon, Ltd.

the other hand, could enjoy 9/10 of an ounce of coffee, or 1/10 of an ounce of tea; the commanding officer dispensed 0.17 pints of spirits, 0.44 pints of wine, or 0.88 pints of beer at his discretion.

The modern piston-driven espresso machine was invented in Milan in 1945 by Achille Gaggia, and from there spread across Italy and the rest of Europe and North America in the early 1950s. With this it was possible to achieve a faster and stronger, more controlled filtration and a better extraction producing an espresso with a rich layer of *crema* – the thin, foamy layer at the top the espresso shot that contains its finest aromas and flavours.

Pino Riservato opened the first espresso bar, the Moka Bar, in London's Soho in 1952; by 1956 there were 400 such bars in London alone. The espresso craze spread across the USA: North Beach in San Francisco was where the Caffè Trieste opened in 1957, which was frequented by Beat Generation writers such as Allen Ginsberg, Jack Kerouac and Bob Kaufman. It was run by Giovanni Giotta who prides himself on getting 'the American people to like cappuccino'. Giotta is also known as 'The Espresso Pioneer', both in Italy and America, because he introduced espresso and cappuccino to the West Coast. Francis Ford Coppola wrote most of the screenplay for *The Godfather* while sipping coffee in the Caffè Trieste. Manhattan's Greenwich Village was another coffee hotspot. In 1927 Café Reggio in the Village installed a La Pavoni espresso machine. First made in 1902, this was the first La Pavoni to be used in the United States.

In 1962 coffee assumed global political status when John F. Kennedy said,

Above and opposite: Four advertisements advertising coffee or coffee essence: *Left*: an 1890 UK trade card; *Right*: a US advert exploiting the fact that many maids were black; *Opposite left*: a 1949 advert from Maxwell House with at least one member of the audience dozing; *Opposite right*: from *Country Gentleman* Magazine, January 1951.

Maxwell House . . . the *one* coffee with that *"Good to the Last Drop" flavor!*

We are attempting to get an agreement on coffee because if we don't get an agreement on coffee we're going to find an increasingly dangerous situation in the coffee-producing countries, and one which would threaten the security of the entire hemisphere.

Later that year, an International Coffee Agreement was negotiated through the United Nations and resulted in worldwide coffee export quotas.

The first Peet's Coffee & Tea store was opened in 1966 in Berkeley, California, by Dutchman Alfred Peet; he became famous for roasting with fresher, higher quality seeds than was usual at the time. Peet was a trainer of and supplier to the founders of Starbucks. Café Trieste had its Beatniks; Peet had his Peetniks.

Starbucks began life as a small business roasting and selling quality coffee beans in 1971 by students Jerry Baldwin, Gordon Bowker and Zev Siegl. Their first shop opened in 1971 in Seattle. Howard Schultz joined in 1982 anxious to sell pre-made espresso coffee. The others were reluctant, but Schultz opened Il Giornale in Seattle in 1986. He bought the other owners out and, from 1987 to the end of 1991, the chain (rebranded from Il Giornale to Starbucks) expanded to over 100 outlets.

George Howell (born 1945), coffee guru, was one of the leaders of the specialty-coffee movement in the United States in the early 1970s. He was the founder of the Coffee Connection, a high-quality coffee retailer based in Boston that was acquired by Starbucks in 1994, and also the founder of the George Howell Terroir Coffee Company. Arriving from the west coast, he said that, 'Boston was a desert of stale, brown-painted wooden pellets and liquefied ground saw dust.' Howell set about putting that right. One of his innovations was roast-dating his coffee beans; coffee unsold after seven days was donated to charity.

A stylish poster promoting Peet's from the 60s designed by Michael Schwab. Peet's patrons were called Peetnicks, as depicted here.

A 1950s advertisement from Folley & Sons of Launceston, Cornwall – coffee 'untouched by hand'.

From its very birth in the Middle East and Ethiopa, coffee has been subjected to prejudice and prohibitions, largely on religious grounds. A contemporary example is in the Church of Jesus Christ of Latter-Day Saints, which maintains that it is both physically and spiritually unhealthy to drink coffee. This derives from the Mormon doctrine of health, given in 1833 by founder Joseph Smith in a revelation called the *Word of Wisdom*. It says that 'hot drinks are not for the belly'; he meant coffee and tea.

Many members of the Seventh-Day Adventist Church also avoid caffeinated drinks. The Church encourages members to avoid tea and coffee and other stimulants. Abstinence has given a virtually unique opportunity for studies to be conducted within that population group on the health effects of coffee drinking, free from complicating factors. One study showed a tenuous but statistically significant association between coffee consumption and mortality from ischemic heart disease, other cardiovascular disease, all cardiovascular diseases combined, and all causes of death.

Among Jews there was an argument over whether the coffee seed was a legume and therefore prohibited for Passover. Maxwell House got involved and in 1923 the coffee seed was classified as a berry rather than a seed by orthodox Jewish rabbi Hersch Kohn, and therefore kosher for Passover.

Kardomah Cafés were a chain of coffee shops in England, Wales, and in Paris, popular from the early 1900s until the 1960s, but now virtually extinct. They featured string quartets. The Kardomah brand began in Pudsey Street, Liverpool, in 1844, as Vey

Top left: Sherlock Holmes and Dr Watson in 1920 enlisted to promote the benefits of Postum, decaffeinated coffee in this US advertisement.

Top right: Betty shows undomesticated husbands how best to make a cup of coffee in this 1940s Australian public service advertisement.

Right: A romantic Bour coffee advert from J. M. Bour Coffee Company, Toledo Ohio.

Brothers tea dealers and grocers. In 1868 the business was acquired by the newly created Liverpool China and India Tea Company, and a series of brands was created beginning with *Mikado. Kardomah* tea was first served at the Liverpool colonial exhibition of 1887, and the brand was extended to a range of teas, coffees and coffee houses. The brand was acquired and anonymised by the Forte Group in 1962, sold to Cadbury/ Schweppes/Typhoo in 1971, and became part of Premier Brands. The brand still exists in instant coffee and coffee whitener. The Paris Kardomah is at 1 Rue de l'Echelle, on the corner of Rue de Rivoli.

Kardomah coffee houses sometimes had their idiosyncrasies. In the 1930s the Swansea branch was the meeting place of the Kardomah Gang, which included Dylan Thomas. In February 1941 Swansea was heavily bombed by the Luftwaffe in a 'Three Nights Blitz' and the Kardomah was destroyed. Dylan Thomas wrote about the devastation in his radio play entitled *Return Journey to Swansea* in which he describes the café as being 'Razed to the snow'.

Liverpool's Kardomah Café, just off Stanley Street was open until the late 1980s and made famous by the song *Kardomah Café* in 1983 by Liverpool group the Cherry Boys. The same branch was also used by the Beatles, and the many Merseybeat groups of the 1960s, who played in the nearby Cavern Club. Milford Kardomah was of course fictional – one of

Life goes on. A fortified Kardomah coffee house in Fleet Street, November 1939.

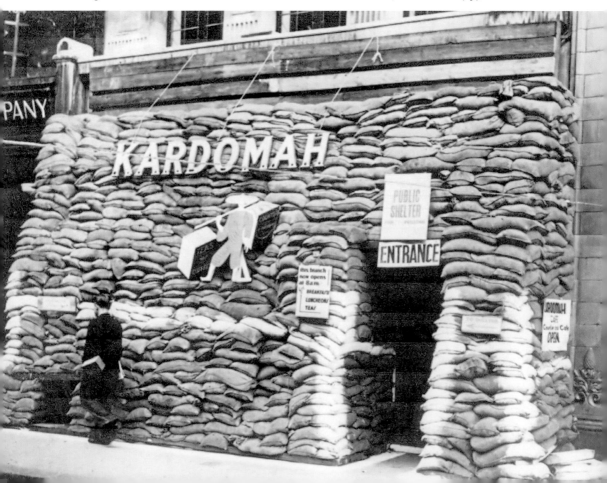

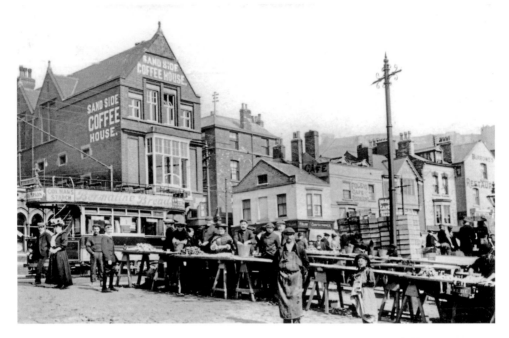

Above: One of the thousands of coffee shops that sprang up in the Edwardian era; this one is at Scarborough. Note the other establishments catering for the tourists.

Right: Anyone for dandelion coffee?

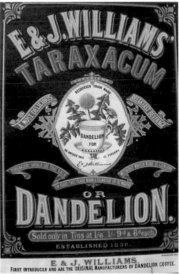

the meeting places used by Alec and Laura in the 1945 film *Brief Encounter* – were it not for the coffee house then the encounters would have been briefer still.

In 1969 Abigail Folger, the heiress to the Folger coffee fortune, was killed by the Manson family at the home of filmmaker Roman Polanski while she was visiting Sharon Tate. In July that year, Apollo 11's LEM Eagle broadcast this to the Johnson Space Center, 'If you'll excuse me a minute, I'm going to have a cup of coffee.' William Burroughs, in *The Adding Machine, Remembering Jack Kerouac* (1985), writes, 'Kerouac opened a million coffee bars and sold a million pairs of Levis to both sexes. Woodstock rises from his pages.'

6

Coffee in Words, Music and Film

Coffee became part of life; it permeated and percolated into world cultures through literature and music. Coffee, like tea, was part of the social fabric, so it is hardly surprising that we see it appearing in words and music from the start of the eighteenth century through to the modern day.

The following is one of the earliest Arabic poems in praise of coffee written about the same time as the first coffee persecution in Mecca (1511):

> In Praise of Coffee
> O Coffee! Thou dost dispel all cares, thou art the object of desire to the scholar.
> This is the beverage of the friends of God; it gives health to those in its service who strive after wisdom. Prepared from the simple shell of the berry, it has the odor of musk and the color of ink.
> The intelligent man who empties these cups of foaming coffee, he alone knows truth.
> May God deprive of this drink the foolish man who condemns it with incurable obstinacy.
> Coffee is our gold. Wherever it is served, one enjoys the society of the noblest and most generous men. O drink! As harmless as pure milk, which differs from it only in its blackness.

John Milton (1608–74) extols coffee in his *Comus*:

> One sip of this
> Will bathe the drooping spirits in delight
> Beyond the bliss of dreams

Coffee is in Alexander Pope's *Rape of the Lock*:

> Coffee (which makes the politician wise,
> And see thro' all things with his half-shut eyes)
> Sent up in vapours to the Baron's brain
> New stratagems, the radiant Lock to gain.

Apparently, Pope (1688–1744) often woke his servant in the middle of the night to make him a cup of coffee; during the day he would normally grind and prepare it on the table. Carruthers' *Life of Pope* tell us that Pope inhaled the steam of coffee in order to ease the headaches to which he was subject. It inspired the following lines:

> As long as Mocha's happy tree shall grow,
> While berries crackle, or while mills shall go;
> While smoking streams from silver spouts shall glide,
> Or China's earth receive the sable tide,
> While coffee shall to British nymphs be dear,
> While fragrant steams the bended head shall cheer,
> Or grateful bitters shall delight the taste,
> So long her honours, name and praise shall last.

Jonathan Swift (1667–1745) teaches us,

> The best Maxim I know in this life is, to drink your Coffee when you can, and when you cannot, to be easy without it. While you continue to be splenetic, count upon it I will always preach. Thus much I sympathize with you that I am not cheerful enough to write, for I believe Coffee once a week is necessary to that.

On the scientific front, Faustus Nairon (Banesius) published the first printed treatise devoted to coffee in Rome, in 1671. The same year, Dufour brought out the first treatise in French, followed in 1684 by *The manner of making coffee, tea, and chocolate*. John Ray praised coffee in his *Universal Botany of Plants*, published in London in 1686. Leonardus Ferdinandus Meisner published a Latin treatise on coffee, tea, and chocolate in 1721. James Douglas released his *A description and History of the Coffee Tree* in London in 1727.

If Susanna Centlivre's 1718 play, *A Bold Strike for a Wife*, is anything to go by, Bohea tea was just as popular in Jonathan's coffee house (where the play was set) as coffee. Henry Fielding (1707–54) published *The Coffee-House Politician, or Justice caught in his own trap*, a comedy, in 1730.

William Cowper (1731–1800) refers to coffee in his *Pity for Poor Africans* in which he is 'shocked at the ignorance of slaves':

> I pity them greatly, but I must be mum
> For how could we do without sugar and rum?
> Especially sugar, so needful we see;
> What! Give up our desserts, our coffee and tea?

William Cobbett (1762–1835) the English-American politician, reformer and writer on economics, denounced coffee as 'slops'; Cobbett, of course, was a through-and-through beer man.

Of the Romantics, Leigh Hunt (1784–1859), and Keats (1795–1834) were both coffee fans; Charles Lamb waxes lyrical on the exploits of Captain de Clieu in *The Coffee Slips*; it starts as follows:

Whene'er I fragrant coffee drink,
I on the generous Frenchman think,
Whose noble perseverance bore
The tree to Martinico's shore.
While yet her colony was new,
Her island products but a few;
Two shoots from off a coffee tree
He carried with him o'er the sea.
Each little tender coffee slip
He waters daily in the ship…

Keats' fantasy, *Cap and Bells*, has the Emperor Elfinan greet Hum, the soothsayer, and offers him a drink:

'You may have sherry in silver, hock in gold, or glass'd champagne
… what cup will you drain?'
'Commander of the Faithful!' answered Hum,
'In preference to these, I'll merely taste
A thimble-full of old Jamaica rum.'
'A simple boon,' said Elfinan; 'thou mayst
Have Nantz, with which my morning coffee's laced.'

Hum accepts the glass of Nantz, without the coffee, 'made racy with the third part of the least drop of crème de citron, crystal clear.'

Leigh Hunt says, 'One of the pleasures we receive in drinking coffee is that, being the universal drink in the East, it reminds of that region of the "Arabian Nights" as smoking does for the same reason'.

Immanuel Kant was extremely fond of coffee in his old age; Thomas de Quincey details Kant's great love of, and grumpy impatience for, the post-prandial cup:

'If it were said, 'Dear Professor, the coffee will be brought up in a moment,' he would say, 'Will be! There's the rub, that it only will be.' Then he would quiet himself with a stoical air, and say, 'Well, one can die after all; it is but dying; and in the next world, thank God, there is no drinking of coffee and consequently no waiting for it.' When the servant's steps were heard upon the stairs, he would turn to us, and joyfully call out: 'Land, land! my dear friends, I see land.'

This is the start of Prior and Montague's vignette inserted in their *City Mouse and Country Mouse*, written in burlesque of Dryden's *Hind and Panther*:

Then on they jogg'd; and since an hour of talk
Might cut a banter on the tedious walk,
As I remember, said the sober mouse,
I've heard much talk of the Wits' Coffee-house;
Thither, says Brindle, thou shalt go and see
Priests supping coffee, sparks and poets tea.

In the second issue of the *Spectator* (1711) Addison tells that:

> I am now settled with a widow woman, who has a great many children and complies with my humour in everything. I do not remember that we have exchanged a word together for these five years; my coffee comes into my chamber every morning without asking for it, if I want fire I point to the chimney, if water, to my basin; upon which my landlady nods as much as to say she takes my meaning, and immediately obeys my signals.

Voltaire, allegedly, but improbably, a fifty-cups-a-day man, wrote *Le Café, ou l'Ecossaise* (1760). Balzac (1799–1850), another avid coffee drinker, has a Philadelphia coffee blend named after him, *La Mort de Balzac*; he also wrote a *Treatise on Modern Stimulants,* in which he linked coffee with imagination and ideas and a remedy for writer's block. His famous white Limoges porcelain coffee pot with the insignia 'HB' can still be seen in the house he rented in Passy in Paris. Thick, Turkish coffee was Balzac's poison – literally; his caffeine abuse was so acute that his physician, Dr Nacquart, attributed Balzac's premature death aged fifty-one to excessive coffee drinking. He used coffee to fuel his nocturnal writing over sixteen to eighteen hours without a break, a regime that could only have aggravated his cardiac hypertrophy. Balzac's vivid description of caffeine in his *Treatise on Modern Stimulants* (see dedication) inspired a series of coffee-colored lino engravings by Pierre Alechinsky, permanently on display in the Balzac museum.

William Makepeace Thackeray (1811–1863), much the wiser from past experience, asks in the *Kickleburys on the Rhine*, 'Why do they always put mud into coffee aboard steamers? Why does the tea generally taste of boiled boots?'

Here we find Jane Austen, an avid tea fan, in Bath obsessing over the coffee accoutrements in a letter to her sister, Cassandra, on June 11 1799: 'It is rather impertinent to suggest any household care to a housekeeper, but I just venture to say that the coffee-mill will be wanted every day while Edward is at Steventon, as he always drinks coffee for breakfast.' Earlier, on 17 May, she hoped that ordering the coffee might cure Edward's fatigue: 'Edward seemed rather fagged last night, and not very brisk this morning; but I trust the bustle of sending for tea, coffee, and sugar, &c., and going out to taste a cheese himself, will do him good.' On 31 May she tells Cassandra that, '[Anna] had a delightful evening with the Miss Middletons -- syllabub, tea, coffee, singing, dancing, a hot supper, eleven o'clock, everything that can be imagined agreeable.' In *Emma*, Miss Bates says: 'No coffee, I thank you, for me – I never take coffee – a little tea if you please.'

Charles Dickens (1812–70) describes his coffee as 'boiling over a charcoal fire, and large slices of bread and butter were piled one upon the other like deals in a lumber yard'. In *Bleak House* we learn that Tom Jarndyce, in despair, committed suicide at a coffee house in Chancery Lane.

In *Household Words*, 12 April 1851, Dickens lampoons Shakespeare in his *The Great Coffee Question* to attack widespread and commonplace adulteration:

> Coffee or chicory - that is the Question. Whether is it better for mankind to suffer the stings and subtleties of outrageous fraud or, by opposing, end them?

Dickens' coffee shop was on the ground floor of his former offices at 26 Wellington Street near Aldwych. The building was also home to the offices for his weekly magazine *All The Year Round*; he also lived in a room in the building after separating from his wife Catherine.

Mark Twain has a lot to say on the matter. In *The Innocents Abroad*, he writes that,

> Of all the unchristian beverages that ever passed my lips, Turkish coffee is the worst. The cup is small, it is smeared with grounds; the coffee is black, thick, unsavory of smell, and execrable in taste. The bottom of the cup has a muddy sediment in it half an inch deep. This goes down your throat, and portions of it lodge by the way, and produce a tickling aggravation that keeps you barking and coughing for an hour.

The following year in *A Tramp Abroad*, things are even worse on the coffee front, the will to live is receding:

> After a few months' acquaintance with European 'coffee' one's mind weakens, and his faith with it, and he begins to wonder if the rich beverage of home, with its clotted layer of yellow cream on top of it, is not a mere dream after all, and a thing which never existed.

According to Agatha Christie, 'Coffee in England always tastes like a chemistry experiment'.

Helen Rowland wrote 'what every wife knows':

> Give me a man who drinks good, hot, dark, strong coffee for breakfast!
> A man who smokes a good, dark, fat cigar after dinner!
> You may marry your milk-faddist, or your anti-coffee crank, as you will!
> But I know the magic of the coffee pot!
> Let me make my Husband's coffee—and I care not who makes eyes at him!
> Give me two matches a day—
> One to start the coffee with, at breakfast, and one for his cigar, after dinner!
> And I defy all the hours in Christendom to light a new flame in his heart!

In 1951 Carson McCullers published her *Ballad of the Sad Café*.

In 1962, writing In the *New York Post*, playwright Christopher Fry states that, 'Coffee in New England is just toasted milk.'

The last words of Bertrand Russell (d. 1970) were 'Life is just one cup of coffee after another, and don't look for anything else.' He was a philosopher, he should know.

Coffee and Cigarettes (October 2004)

This is a short cult black-and-white film comprising eleven comic vignettes that have coffee and cigarettes as a common theme. In each, the stars play semi-fictionalised versions of themselves and meet in a diner where they talk about coffee and cigarettes, the fact that caffeine and nicotine are unhealthy, especially if that is all you have for lunch. These meetings for the consumption of coffee or tea and cigarettes are a vehicle to overcome arguments and uncomfortable situations. Also discussed are delirium, the relationship between musicians and doctors, industrial music, and drinking coffee before sleeping to induce exciting dreams. Iggy Pop, Tom Waits, Cate Blanchett, Jack White, Steve Coogan and Bill Murray all feature in the cast. The film was shot over seventeen years, Roberto Benigni and Steven Wright were filmed in 1986, but Tom Waits and Iggy Pop were not filmed until 1995.

Blackadder the Third (1987)

Coffee features quite a lot in the third series of Richard Curtis's and Ben Elton's comedy hit *Blackadder*. Mrs. Miggins runs a coffee shop and serves a liquid that Blackadder describes as 'brown grit in hot water'. In 'Nob and Nobility', Blackadder and Baldrick visit the shop and stumble upon Le Comte de Frou Frou, who is in fact a disguised Lord Topper (the Scarlet Pimpernel). In 'Sense and Senility', Blackadder and Baldrick return to the coffee shop to meet two actors. In 'Ink and Incapability', Blackadder and Baldrick revisit the shop to meet Dr Samuel Johnson, only to find Johnson with three poets. The poets tell them they are dying, but Mrs Miggins banishes their concerns when she assures them that they are not really dying, 'they are being intellectual'. Mrs Miggins next features when Blackadder visits her coffee shop to meet his Scottish cousin MacAdder. MacAdder, instead of helping his cousin, proposes to Mrs Miggins and they run off together.

One More Cup of Coffee for the Road

Given the association between the performance and composition of popular music and the long days and nights associated with this, it is hardly surprising that coffee, stimulant that it is, gets name-checked frequently. Here is an utterly incomplete and entirely subjective list of truly eclectic songs united only by a mention of coffee.

Coffee gets a part in Tchaikovsky's *Nutcracker Suite* in Act II Scene 1: *The Land of Sweets*. When Clara and the Prince travel to the Land of Sweets, a celebration of sweets from around the world is produced: chocolate from Spain, coffee from Arabia, and tea from China.

In 1932, Irving Berlin wrote, 'Just around the corner, there's a rainbow in the sky, so let's have another cup o' coffee, and let's have another piece o' pie.' From *Let's Have Another Cup of Coffee* in the musical comedy *Face the Music*.

Sting's 1987 prim 'I don't drink coffee, I take tea, my dear' from *Englishman in New York*, is based on the life of quintessential exiled Englishman; *One Cup of Coffee* by Bob Marley is upbeat for a divorce song , but no one can be that depressed when they're sipping Jamaican coffee; In *Caffeine* Patty Larkin name-drops George Howell's Harvard Square café, the Coffee Connection (birthplace of the frappuccino) in this 1985 blues tune; In *Will You?* Hazel O'Connor has him drinking coffee while she sips her tea and wonders whether he will get her into bed.

7

It's the Coffee Talking:
Some Famous Coffee Quotations

Behind every successful woman is a substantial amount of coffee.

Stephanie Piro

I never drink coffee at lunch. I find it keeps me awake for the afternoon.

Ronald Reagan

If this is coffee, then please bring me some tea. But if this is tea,
please bring me some coffee.

Abraham Lincoln

In Seattle you haven't had enough coffee until you can thread a sewing machine while
it's running.

Jeff Bezos

Caffeine is my shepherd; I shall not doze.
It maketh me to wake in green pastures:
It leadeth me beyond the sleeping masses.
It restoreth my buzz:
It leadeth me in the paths of consciousness for its name's sake.
Yea, though I walk through the valley of the shadow of addiction…
…my mug runneth over.
Surely richness and taste shall follow me all the days of my life:
And I will dwell in the House of Mochas forever.

Anonymous

I have measured out my life with coffee spoons.

T. S. Eliot

Ah! How sweet coffee tastes! Lovelier than a thousand kisses, sweeter far
than muscatel wine!

'Coffee Cantata', J. S. Bach

I never laugh until I've had my coffee.

Clark Gable

You can tell when you have crossed the frontier into Germany because of the badness of the coffee.

Edward VII

Decaf is like masturbating with an oven mitt!

Robin Williams

There are three intolerable things in life - cold coffee, lukewarm champagne, and overexcited women …

Orson Welles

Probably the best quotation of them all.

8

Coffee and Health:
Elixir or Poison?

Controversy has raged around coffee and its alleged health benefits – or otherwise – since people started to drink it. In that respect it is no different from tea, chocolate and cocoa, which suffered the same indignities, and still do to some extent.

The original poster advertising Pasqual Rosée's coffee house proclaimed that coffee was 'to be drunk, fasting half an hour before, and not eating an hour after, and to be taken as hot as possibly can be endured; the which will never take the skin off the mouth, or raise any blisters by reason of that heat'. It also cured disorders including 'Defluxions of Rhumes [runny nose], Dropsy [oedema], Gout, Scurvy, King's-evil [scrofula] and Spleen'.

In Britain, alleged cures for 'Head-Melancholy' (hang-over headache), gout, scurvy, smallpox and excessive inebriation were ascribed to coffee. In the opposite camp, though, some believed that excessive coffee consumption could result in languor, paralysis, heart disease and trembling limbs, as well as depression and anxiety disorders.

King Gustav III of Sweden (1746–92) wanted to prove that coffee was a poison, so ordered a convicted murderer to drink coffee every day until he died. To make the experiment more scientific, he ordered another murderer to drink tea daily, with two Swedish doctors monitoring the experiment. Things did not go well for Gustav: the two murderers lived long lives in prison – the tea drinker lived to the age of eighty-three while the coffee drinker died at an even older age. The prisoners outlived the doctors and King Gustav, who was murdered.

What Charles W. Trigg said in his 1920 *Pharmacology of Coffee* still holds good today:

> Published information regarding the effects of coffee drinking on the human system is so contradictory in its nature that it is hazardous to make many generalizations about the physiological behavior of coffee.

At one extreme, coffee is the elixir of life; at the other, a poison. Many contemporary reports on coffee and health are of dubious value and even of more doubtful provenance. However, the centre of excellence Mayo Clinic has this to say on its website:

> Recent studies have generally found no connection between coffee and an increased risk of cancer or heart disease. In fact, most studies find an association between coffee consumption and decreased overall mortality and possibly cardiovascular

mortality, although this may not be true in younger people who drink large amounts of coffee.

Studies have shown that coffee may have health benefits, including protecting against Parkinson's disease, type 2 diabetes and liver disease, including liver cancer. It also appears to improve cognitive function and decrease the risk of depression. However, the research appears to bear out some risks. High consumption of unfiltered coffee (boiled or espresso) has been associated with mild elevations in cholesterol levels.

(From http://www.mayoclinic.org/healthy-lifestyle/nutrition-and-healthy-eating/expert-answers/coffee-and-health/faq-20058339; accessed 11 June 2015)

There does appear to be agreement that moderate coffee consumption is good for headaches, in combination with a painkiller. As with many things, moderate consumption is fine for the vast majority of people.

Trigg explains the stimulatory effects of coffee:

The ingestion of coffee infusion is always followed by evidences of stimulation. It acts upon the nervous system as a powerful cerebro-spinal stimulant, increasing mental activity and quickening the power of perception, thus making the thoughts more precise and clear, and intellectual work easier without any evident subsequent depression. The muscles are caused to contract more vigorously, increasing their working power without there being any secondary reaction leading to a diminished capacity for work. Its action upon the circulation is somewhat antagonistic; for while it tends to increase the rate of the heart by acting directly on the heart muscle, it tends to decrease it by stimulating the inhibitory center in the medulla.

Likewise, its effect as a diuretic:

The effect on the kidneys is more marked, the diuretic effect being shown by an increase in water, soluble solids, and of uric acid directly attributable to the caffeine content of the coffee taken.

Il Fiori coffee house in Turin. (Courtesy of Giallo Magenta Cano, Studio Fotografico Moncalieri, Torino Daniele Terragni)

Tea and chocolate were endlessly adulterated; a similar crime was visited on coffee with the regular use of old coffee grounds: these were mixed with sand, gravel, and chicory and dandelions. Chicory itself was often polluted by roasted carrots and turnips to create the aroma, with a sprinkling of 'black jack' (burnt sugar) to lend it that rich coffee colour. Seamen on Royal Navy ships made substitute coffee by dissolving burnt bread in hot water.

A didactic poster from Camp Coffee of Glasgow, teaching the lessons of health, prosperity and wisdom which their flavoursome, unadulterated coffee essence imbues. It was developed in 1885 as a thick black syrup, a 'secret blend' of sugar, water, coffee and chicory essence and came in a square, eight-and-a-half fluid-ounce glass bottle, a bit like the HP Sauce bottle. The Camp website takes up the story: 'The original label showed a moustachioed Gordon Highlander sitting on a cushion drinking a cup of Camp, while a turbaned Sikh servant stood patiently next to him, holding a tray with a bottle of Camp and a jug. A tent in the background was topped by a fluttering pennant with the words 'Ready Aye Ready.' This labeling was controversial: 'Major General Sir Hector McDonald was the model for the Gordon Highlander. The son of a crofter, he had worked his way up through the ranks, serving in the Afghan War and in India [and was known as] 'Fighting Mac' ... he was wounded in the second Boer War and later given command of the regiment's troops in Ceylon {Sri Lanka] where charges of homosexuality were brought against him ... he shot himself in a Paris hotel in 1903 ... it was complaints of racism, allegedly from Asian shopkeepers, that led [in 2006 to] the new label show[ing] the officer and the Sikh sitting side by side, both drinking Camp, an excellent example now of racial equality and historical revisionism.'

9

Twenty-First-Century Coffee

A conundrum: coffee shops are enjoying a sales growth of 10.7 per cent, but coffee consumption in the UK is down. This coffee shop high is accounted for by the fact that 85 per cent of us apparently visit a coffee shop at least once a week, consuming an estimated 2 billion cups of coffee per year. Both figures look suspiciously high but are supported by Project Café 2015 UK – the Allegra World Coffee Portal report www.worldcoffeeportal.com – which also forecasts 'the turnover of UK coffee shops to reach £16.5 billion by 2020 across 27,000 outlets'. An increase of over 8,000 outlets in the next five years is expected, generating an increase of £9.3 billion profit.

> Costa Coffee, Starbucks Coffee Company and Caffè Nero represent a combined 56 per cent of the branded chain market by outlet numbers – some 5,781 operating at a £2.9 billion turnover in 2014. This figure includes the opening of 271 new coffee shops, 151 of which were Costa Coffee – selling the most cups at 149 million.

We have Costa to thank for the UK coffee revolution in 1995. When Whitbread bought Costa Coffee, coffee became widely available again on the high street. McDonalds took second place in most cups of coffee sold last year at 126 million.

Levels of coffee drunk today are lower than they were in 2006. We consume a modest 2.8 kg per head compared to France, where the figure is 5.5 kg. In Germany they consume 7 kg and the figure is 7.1 kg in Sweden.

The critical change is that we're now going out to drink it rather than making instant coffee at home or at work. Socialising in coffee shops is now the thing to do; coffee shop visits by women have made the significant difference, just as they did in the tea houses and tea shops in the earlier part of the twentieth century. The growth in female social independence and the concomitant increase in female spending power have contributed. Now, over half of Costa customers are women. Online shopping has helped as well; instead of spending Saturdays and Sundays trooping round the shops, we now have the time to meet up with friends at, or take the family to, a coffee shop. Disposable time as well as disposable income. The market in the UK recorded a 6.4 per cent increase in sales in 2013 when there were 16,501 coffee shops across the UK.

Coffee knowledge has also helped with enhanced fluency in origin, roasting, milk frothing and water quality. Some of us are now coffee connoisseurs, increasingly obsessive about quality, and choice – and taste. Good, individualistic, atmospheric artisan coffee shops are fuelling that growth, as well as those faceless, anytown chains.

The twenty-first-century trend of melding bookshops (those that are left) with coffee shops is simply a contemporary revival of an old custom. We have seen how coffee houses and coffee drinking enjoyed an association with printing and publishing – not just of newspapers, but of books and magazines too. The printed word is what they had, and have again, in common. In the late seventeenth and eighteenth century the blossoming of the coffee shop coincided with the Restoration and the sweeping away of all the cultural privations imposed by the Puritans; and then the enlightenment came along with its world-changing developments in geography, science and philosophy. Look at the clientele in today's coffee shops and what do you see? Readers, books, newspapers, tablets and laptops – another coffee-sipping social, cultural and information revolution in full swing.

Death Cafés are a new social phenomenon. At a Death Café people drink coffee or tea, eat cake and discuss death. Their aim is to increase awareness of death to help people make the most of their (finite) lives. Death Cafés have spread quickly across Europe, North America and Australasia. As of today, over 2,093 impromptu social franchise Death Cafés have popped up around the world since September 2011. Organisers claim that people are keen to talk about death and that many are passionate enough to organise their own Death Café. Where better to drink a cup of the devil's drink?

A scene inside Bettys in York in 2015. The tablet has superseded the seventeenth-century newsheets and pamphlets, but the coffee shop information revolution goes on just the same.

A darker side of coffee with this funereal, erotic advertisement promoting *Le Macabre* coffee shop in London's Soho with its beatnik goth interior in the 1960s. *Le Macabre* enjoyed the distinction of being one of two horror-themed cafés in the UK. It had coffins as tables and Bakelite skulls for ashtrays, skull-shaped milk jugs, murals of skeletons and graveyards, a ghoulish jukebox selection of chthonic records including Chopin's *Funeral March*. Regulars included local legends such as Iron Foot Jack, who sported a real iron foot. Just around the corner was *Heaven & Hell*, with its resident skiffle group called The Ghouls who performed in a hell basement painted completely black.

Finally, Some Instant Facts

On average in the west, coffee consumption is about a third of that of tap water, so for every three cups of water you drink, someone somewhere will be having a cup of coffee.

After petroleum, coffee is the second most traded commodity in the world.

Over 7 million metric tons are produced annually.

Tap water apart, coffee is the most popular drink worldwide, with over 400 billion cups drunk each year.

The market in the UK recorded a 6.4 per cent increase in sales in 2013; there were 16,501 coffee shops across the UK by the end of last year. Even with fifteen years already of continuous rapid expansion, Britain's coffee shop sector still remains one of the most successful in the UK economy and continues to grow. Coffee shops are part of the fabric of British society now.

In 2011, UK consumers retail spend on coffee was £941 million. The average spend in a coffee shop continues to rise and consumers are also visiting coffee shops more: in 2010 one in nine people visited a coffee shop every day. That has risen to one in five people in 2015.

In the UK we drink approximately 70 million cups of coffee per day.

In 2011 UK consumers retail spend on coffee was £941 million.

In 2012 the estimated turnover for UK coffee shops was £5.8 billion (including non-coffee lines).

In 2015 about 1.7 billion cups of coffee were sold in the UK from more than 18,000 outlets; this is set to grow to 21,000 by 2020, according to Allegra Strategies.

Almost three-quarters (74 per cent) of all UK adults drink instant coffee, compared to around half (48%) who drink fresh coffee (i.e. ground/full bean coffee or coffee pods). As you'll have worked out, some drink both.

In the UK we consume over 500 g of coffee per person, per year.

In 2015 Costa was the market leader, with 2,000 stores in the UK and like-for-like growth of 6 per cent for the fifty weeks to 12 February. The Whitbread-owned chain has plans to open another 250 stores worldwide from 2015 to 2016.

Pubs are getting in on the act with low grade but high taste coffee, and even the baker Greggs is investing more in coffee. Between 2015 and 2017 refurbishing the remaining 400 stores of its 1,650 estate will be completed to offer coffee on the go. In 2014 Greggs sold £1m-worth of coffee every week.

In March 2015 JD Wetherspoon stirred up the coffee price war by cutting the price of its Lavazza filter coffee to 99p, with free refills. The company now sells almost 1 million coffees a week largely because more people visit their pubs for breakfast than Prêt A Manger or Caffè Nero, according to CGA Peach. 'By the end of 2016, chairman Tim Martin aims to triple its coffee and breakfast sales, further blurring the distinction between pub and coffee shop.'

Fuller's, the brewery and pub chain, sells more than 1.25 million cups a year; they opened a coffee shop in October 2014 to train its staff as baristas.

Over half of the espresso consumed in the UK is drunk in the south-east corner of the country.

On average, UK men drink more coffee than women (1.7 cups per day versus 1.5 cups).

37 per cent of UK coffee drinkers drink their coffee black; while 63 per cent add a sweetener such as sugar.

In the UK 57 per cent of all coffee drunk is drunk at breakfast; 34 per cent between meals and 13 per cent at other meals.

Two-thirds of UK consumers actually buy coffee or other hot drinks outside of the home, and this rises to three in four among sixteen to twenty-four-year-olds.

Coffee is grown in around eighty countries, clustered around the equator in Latin America, Southeast Asia, and Africa.

Central and South America produce approximately two-thirds of the world's coffee supply.

The main suppliers of coffee in the world are Brazil, Colombia and Vietnam, with Brazil contributing around 30 per cent of the total.

The word 'coffee' comes from the Ottoman Turkish 'kahve'. It became an English word in 1582 via the Dutch *koffie*, borrowed from *kahve*, in turn borrowed from the Arabic *qahwah* (قوه).

The world consumes nearly 1.6 billion cups or mugs of coffee per day.

Coffee is *the* vital cash crop for many developing countries. Over 100 million people are dependent on coffee as their primary source of income. It is the primary export and economic bedrock for countries like Uganda, Burundi, Rwanda and Ethiopia, as well as for many Central American countries.

It takes forty-two coffee beans to make an espresso.

Caffeine is the world's most widely consumed psychoactive drug. Global consumption of caffeine has been estimated at 120,000 tonnes per year. This amounts to one serving of a caffeinated beverage for every person every day.

A cup of coffee contains 80–175 mg of caffeine, depending on what bean is used and how it is prepared (e.g. drip, percolation, or espresso). So, you would need about fifty to 100 regular cups of coffee to reach a lethal dose.

The human body will absorb just 300 mg of caffeine at a given time. Additional amounts are cast off and provide no additional stimulation. The human body dissipates 20 per cent of the caffeine in its system per hour.

Espresso contains less caffeine than any other roast.

In Thailand Black Ivory coffee beans are fed to elephants, whose digestive enzymes eradicate most of the bitter taste of the beans. The beans are carefully collected from their dung and sold for up to $1,100 a kilogram making it the most expensive blend in the world. A different blend, Kopi Luwak, goes through a similar process after the beans are eaten by the Asian Palm Civet; unfortunately, these only fetch $600 a kilo.

It is estimated that more than 100 million Americans drink a total of 350 million cups of coffee a day.

The USA is the world's largest consumer of coffee, importing 16 to 20 million bags annually (2.5 million lb), representing one-third of all coffee exported. More than half of the United States population consumes coffee, typically drinking 3.4 cups of coffee a day.

Coffee represents three-quarters of all the caffeine consumed in the USA.

American coffee consumers spent about $165 each on coffee during the year, on average.

The first European coffee was sold in pharmacies in 1615 as a medicinal remedy.

Cappuccino may be named because of the drink's peak of foam, which resembles the cowl of a Capuchin friar's habit.

Coffee was first known in Europe as Arabian Wine.

The US Navy used to serve alcoholic beverages on board ships. However, when Admiral Josephus 'Joe' Daniels became Chief of Naval Operations, he outlawed alcohol on board ships, except for very special occasions. Coffee then became the drink of choice, hence the term 'cup of Joe'.

Italians do not drink espresso during meals. It is considered to be a separate event and is given its own time.

In Greece and Turkey, the oldest person is almost always served their coffee first.

Raw coffee beans, soaked in water and spices, are chewed in many parts of Africa.

The Japanese bathe in coffee grounds fermented with pineapple pulp to reduce wrinkles and improve their skin.

The Europeans added chocolate to their coffee in the 1600s.

The French philosopher, Voltaire, reportedly drank fifty cups of coffee a day. Myth.

Decaffeinated coffee sales are at their highest in January due to people's New Year resolutions.

Iced coffee in a can has been popular in Japan since 1945.

South Korea had almost 900 per cent growth in the number of coffee shops between 2006 and 2011. The capital Seoul now has the highest concentration of coffee shops in the world, with more than 10,000 cafes and coffee houses.

Regular coffee drinkers have about 33 per cent fewer asthma symptoms than those of non-coffee drinkers according to a Harvard researcher who studied 20,000 people.

Australians consume 60 per cent more coffee than tea, a six-fold increase since 1940.

Turkish law makes it legal for a woman to divorce her husband if he fails to provide her with her daily quota of coffee.

In 2010 a car fuelled by coffee travelled 250 miles from London to Manchester. Known as the 'Car-puccino', it was fuelled by the equivalent of 11,000 espressos.

It was apparently the coffee houses of England that started the custom of tipping waiters and waitresses (although tea competes for this honour too). People who wanted good service and better seating would put some money in a tin labelled 'To Insure Prompt Service' – hence 'TIPS'.

The 2011 Guinness World Record of the most coffee beans moved with chopsticks in one minute was won by Cynthia Nojicic, who moved thirty-eight beans.

The largest cup of coffee containing 13,200 litres won the Guinness World Record in London in 2012.

Astronauts in the International Space Station finally get a decent cup of coffee with the first espresso machine in space in 2014.

European countries rated for their approximate coffee consumption per capita (in kgs):

1	Finland	12.82
2	Denmark	12.33
3	Sweden	11.9
4	Holland	10.2
5	Belgium	9.67
5	Norway	9.67
7	Switzerland	9.36
8	Germany	7.32
9	Austria	6.41
10	France	5.75
11	Italy	4.8
12	Hungary	2.2
13	Greece	2.12
14	Spain	1.86
15	UK	1.76
16	Portugal	1.37

New research on the coffee and coffee shop sectors in the UK has been released. [All figures relating to the commissioned research remain the copyright of Allegra Strategies and Beyond the Bean: UK Iced ©Allegra & Beyond the Bean: UK Iced Beverage Market – Strategic Analysis 2014]

Further Reading
(With One More Cup of Coffee)

Allen, S. L., *The Devil's Cup: Coffee, the Driving Force in History* (London, 1999)

Anonymous, *Old English Coffee Houses* (London, 1954)

Anonymous, *A Number of Pamphlets: Many Scandalous, Seditious and Unlicensed* (Norwich, 1968)

Arvidson, E. *Bean Business Basics* Third Edition (New York, 2013)

Barr, A. *Drink, A Social History* (London, 1995)

Bartley, D.C., *Adulteration of Food: Statutes, Cases and Regulations 4th ed* (London, 1929)

Bennett A. W., *The World of Caffeine: The Science and Culture of the World's Most Popular Drug* (London, 2001)

Berichevsky, N., *Coffee Or Tea? The Cultural Geography of Consumption* (2008) http://www.newenglishreview.org/custpage.cfm/frm/9972/sec_id/9972 accessed 8.3.2014

Berry, H., Rethinking Politeness in Eighteenth-Century England: Moll King's Coffee House and the Significance of 'Flash Talk', *Transactions of the Royal Historical Society* 11: 65–81, (2001)

Boyer, M. F., *The French Café*. London, 1994)

Bramah, E., *Tea & Coffee: a Modern View of Three Hundred Years of Tradition* (London, 1972)

Brandon, D., *Life in a Seventeenth-Century Coffee Shop* (Stroud, 2007)

Brown, P. B., *In Praise of Hot Liquors: The Study of Chocolate, Coffee and Tea-drinking, 1600–1850* (York, 1995)

Burford, E. J., *Wits, Wenchers and Wantons – London's Low Life: Covent Garden in the Eighteenth Century.* (London, 1986)

Burn, J. H., *A Descriptive Catalogue of the London traders, Tavern, and Coffee-house Toke. 2nd ed.* (London, 1869)

Burnett, J., *The History of Food Adulteration in Great Britain in the Nineteenth Century, with Special Reference to Bread, Tea and Beer* (Diss. U of London, 1958)

Burnett, J., *Plenty and Want: A Social History of Diet in England from 1815 to the Present Day* (London, 1979)

Burnett, J., *Liquid Pleasures: A Social History of Drinks in Modern Britain* (London, 1999)

Carter, H., *The English Temperance Movement 1830–1899* (London, 1933)

Cheney, R. H., *Coffee: A Monograph of the Economic Species of the Genus* Coffea L. (New York, 1925)

Chrystal, P., *Chocolate: A History* (London, 2011)

Chrystal, P., *A History of Chocolate in York* (Barnsley, 2012)

Chrystal, P., *York Industries* (Stroud, 2012)

Chrystal, P., *The Rowntree Family: A Social History* (Pickering, 2013)

Chrystal, P., *Tea: A Very British Beverage* (Stroud, 2014)

Cornelis, M. C., 'Coffee, Caffeine, and Coronary Heart Disease'. *Current Opinion in Clinical Nutrition and Metabolic Care* 10.6 (2007): 745–751

Cowan, B. W.,*The Social Life of Coffee: The Emergence of the British Coffeehouse*, (London, 2005)

Cowan, B. W., 'What Was Masculine about the Public Sphere? Gender and the Coffeehouse Milieu in Post-Restoration England.' *History Workshop Journal* 51(2001): 127-157.

Denyer, C.H., 'The Consumption of Tea and Other Staple Drinks', *The Economic Journal* 3.9(1983), 33–51

Dix, G., 'Non-Alcoholic Beverages in Nineteenth-Century Russia'. *Petits Propos Culinaires* 10 (1982): 21–28

Ellis, A., *The Penny Universities: A History of the Coffee-Houses* (London, 1956)

Ellis, J., *An Historical Account of Coffee* (Cambridge, 2013)

Ellis, M., *The Coffee-house: A Cultural History* (London, 2004)

Flanders, J., *Consuming Passions: Leisure and Pleasure in Victorian Britain* (London, 2011)

Fraser, W. H., *The Coming of the Mass Market 1850–1914* (London, 1981)

Freedman, N. D., (2012). 'Association of Coffee Drinking with Total and Cause-Specific Mortality'. *New England Journal of Medicine* 366 (20): 1891–1904

Galland, A., *De l'origine et du Progrez du Café*, Éd. originale J. Cavelie (Paris, 1992)

Haine, W. S., *The World of the Paris Café: Sociability among the French Working Class, 1789–1914* (Baltimore, 1998)

Halliwell-Phillipps, J.O. The Jokes of the Cambridge Coffee Houses in *Cambridge Jokes from the 17th to the 20th Century* (Cambridge 2009)

Harris, J., 'The Grecian coffee house and political debate in London, 1688-1714', *The London Journal* 25 (2000), 1–13

Hattox, R. S., *Coffee and Coffeehouses: The Origins of a Social Beverage in the Medieval Near East* (Seattle, 1988)

Janes, H., *Two Centuries: The Story of David Lloyd Pigott and Company of London, Tea and Coffee Merchants, 1760–1960* (London, 1960)

Kaye, A. S., (1986). 'The etymology of "coffee": The dark brew'. *Journal of the American Oriental Society* 106 (3): 557–558.

Keay, J., *The Honourable Company: A History of the English East India Company* (London, 1991)

Klein, L. E., 'Coffeehouse Civility, 1660-1714: An Aspect of Post-Courtly Culture in England'. *The Huntington Library Quarterly* 59, (1996). 30–51.

Lawson, P., *The East India Company: A History* (London, 1993)

Lillywhite, B., *The London Coffee Houses: A Reference Book of Coffee Houses of the Seventeenth, Eighteenth, and Nineteenth Centuries* (London, 1963)

Markman, E., (2001). 'Coffee-women, The Spectator and the public sphere in early eighteenth century'. In Eger, E., *Women, Writing and the Public Sphere, 1700–1830.* (Cambridge, 2001), 27–52

Matthee, R., Exotic substances: The introduction and global spread of tobacco, coffee, tea, and distilled liquor, 16th to 18th centuries', in *Drugs and Narcotics in History*, ed. R. Porter (Cambridge, 1995), 24–51

Milletto, B, *Effective & Essential Marketing for the Specialty Coffee Retailer 2nd Edition*, (New York, 2013)

Morrow, W.C., 'The Café Procope' in *Bohemian Paris of Today* (1900), 207–220

O'Connor, J. J., 'London Coffee houses and mathematics': www history.mcs st-and. ac.uk/HistTopics/Coffee_houses.html. Retrieved 19 June 2015

Oldenburg, R., *The Great Good Place: Cafes, Coffee Shops, Community Centers, General Stores, Bars, Hangouts, and How They Get You through the Day.* (New York, 1989)

Park, K. 'Coffeehouses and Print Shops' in *The Cambridge History of Science Volume 3: Early Modern Science* (Cambridge) 320–340

Pelzer, J. Coffee Houses of Augustan London. *History Today* (1982), 40–47Pendergrast, M. (2001) *Uncommon Grounds: The History of Coffee and How It Transformed Our World* (London 2001)

Pelzer, J., 'Coffee: Second to Oil?' in *Tea & Coffee Trade Journal* (April 2009), 38–41

Pincus, S., 'Coffee Politicians does Create: Coffeehouses and Restoration Political Culture', *Journal of Modern History*, 67 (1995), 807–834

Robinson, E. F., *The Early History of Coffee Houses in England* (1893 original, reprinted. Cambridge, 2013)

Shelley, H.C., 'Inns and Taverns of Old London Part IV: Pleasure Gardens of Old London': www.buildinghistory.org/primary/inns/gardens.shtml. Retrieved 19 June 2015

Shelley, H. C., 'Coffee-houses of old London': http://www.buildinghistory.org/primary/inns/coffee-houses.shtml. Retrieved 19.6.2015

Sherman, S., 'Impotence and Capital: The Debate over Imported Beverages in the Seventeenth and Eighteenth Centuries', *1650–1850: Ideas, Aesthetics, and Inquiries in the Early Modern Era: vol. 9*, ed. K. L. Cope, (New York 2003) p. 142.

Schivelbusch, W. *Tastes of Paradise: A Social History of Spices, Stimulants, and Intoxicants*, trans. D. Jacobson, (New York 1992)

Smith, W. D., 'From Coffee-house to Parlour: The consumption of coffee, tea, and sugar in north-western Europe in the seventeenth and eighteenth centuries', in J. Goodman (ed.), *Consuming Habits: deconstructing drugs in history and anthropology* (London, 1995), 148–163.

Somerville, C. J., 'Surfing the Coffeehouse', *History Today* 47 (1997), 8–10

Standage, T., *A History of the World in 6 Glasses* (London, 2007)

Steensgaard, N., *The Asian Trade Revolution of the Seventeenth Century: The East India Companies and the Decline of the Caravan Trade* (Chicago, 1975)

Stewart, L., 'Other centres of Calculation, or, Where the Royal Society Didn't Count: Commerce, Coffee-houses and Natural Philosophy in Early Modern London', *British Journal for the History of Science*, 32 (1999), 133–53.

Sussman, C., *Consuming Anxieties: Consumer Protest, Gender and British Slavery, 1713–1833* (Stanford, 2000)

Varey, S. 'Three Necessary Drugs' [Coffee, tea and chocolate], in K. Cope (ed.), *1650–1850: Ideas, Aesthetics, and Inquiries in the Early Modern Era* (New York, 1998), IV, 3–51

Teply, K., *The Introduction of Coffee in Vienna* (Vienna, 1980)

Thesiger, W., A Journey Through the Tihama, the 'Asir, and the Hijaz Mountains. *The Geographical Journal*, 110, No. 4/6 (Oct–Dec, 1947), 192

Toussaint-Samat, M., *A History of Food 2nd edition* (2008), 'Coffee in Legend', 532–534

Ukers, W., *All About Coffee* (New York 1935)

Walvin, James, *Fruits of Empire: Exotic Produce and British Taste, 1660–1800* (London, 1997)

Weatherill, L., *Consumer Behaviour and Material Culture in Britain, 1660–1760* (London, 1988)

Weatherstone, J., *The Pioneers, 1825–1900: The Early British Tea and Coffee Planters & Their Way of Life* (London, 1986)

Weinberg, B. A., *The World of Caffeine* (New York, 2001)

Wessells, H., *Ambrosia Arabica: Books and Coffee in History*. Originally published in *AB Bookman's Weekly,* 15 December 1997

White, E. (ed.), *Feeding a City: York* (Totnes, 2000)

Wild, A., (2004) *Coffee: A Dark History*

Wild, J., *Hearts, Tarts & Rascals: The Story of Bettys* (Harrogate, 2005)

Yaşar, A., 'The Coffeehouses in Early Modern Istanbul: Public Space, Sociability and Surveillance', MA Thesis, Boğaziçi Üniversitesi, 2003: http://seyhan.library.boun.edu.tr/search/aya%7B240%7Dsar%2C+ahmet/ayas~aar+ahmet/1%2C1%2C3%2CB/frameset&FF=ayas~aar+ahmet+1978&2%2C%2C3. Retrieved 19 June 2015

Acknowledgements

My thanks to the following for allowing permission to use their images: Sarah Wells at Bettys and Taylors of Harrogate Ltd; Alberto Landi, Bicerin in Turin; Paola Francesca Bordonaro, Caffè Fiorio in Turin; Agata Donà, Caffè Florian in Venice; Steve Lewis, York Press.

Index